Hooked on Baja

Hooked on Baja

Where & How to Fish Mexico's Legendary Waters

Tom Gatch

The Countryman Press
Woodstock, Vermont

Dedication

This book is dedicated to the two most important ladies
in my life: my loving mother, Florence, and my wonderful wife,
Lynn, without whom this book would never have been
possible. This book and the spirit of the information herein
are also dedicated to my dad, Dave Gatch, who was
the first person in my life to have the vision and sense
to put a fishing rod in my hand.

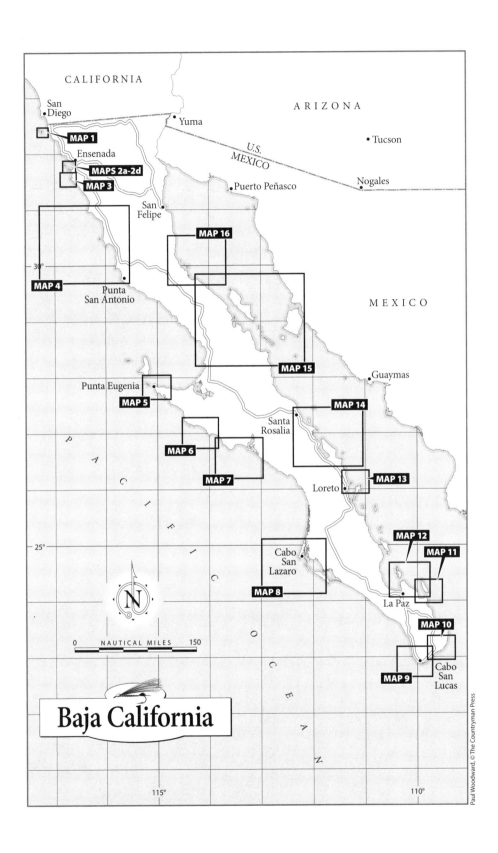

Baja California

Contents

Introduction

The Magic of Baja

Come with me to a magical place where the sun shines practically year-round and squadrons of hungry pelicans cruise mere inches above the surface of the ocean each morning in search of their breakfast. It is a land that is almost completely surrounded by seas that range in color from light turquoise to a deep, intense indigo.

This is a welcoming region that is rich in ancient culture, friendly people, and a sense of freedom often difficult to find in the hectic, frenzied urban environments in which many of us spend most of our lives today.

Americans need not fly halfway around the world to sit under these palm trees, as pods of dolphin surface momentarily to catch a breath while swimming parallel to the breakers just off the beach. Warm, arid breezes caress those who lie on the sand near the shore while inland, a sometimes blistering sun brings to life an exotic array of cacti and succulents, several of which can be found nowhere else on our planet.

The name of this legendary peninsula is Baja California.

The oceans surrounding Baja possess a richer and more diverse population of marine life than can be found anywhere else along Mexico's entire shoreline. Off its western coast, the vast Pacific Ocean provides access to a wide variety of migratory fish species such as yellowfin, bluefin, and bigeye tuna, wahoo, amberjack, and yellowtail, as well as to a host of colder-water species, some of which are members of the rockfish genus, *Sebastes,* commonly known as "rock cod."

Along the eastern coast of Baja lies the Sea of Cortez, which was originally made famous by legendary writer Ray Cannon, who often referred to it as an angler's paradise. Many warmwater fishes such as tropical grouper, corvina, pompano, pargo, and dorado abound in this tepid, desert sea. Near the southern tip, there is a merging of species that often extends a short distance up the coast in each direction.

In addition to providing extensive information on how to get the most out of your Baja California experience, this book will also focus on the great fishing to be found along both coasts of the peninsula. You will learn the best ways to take advantage of an opportunity to experience the kind of angling and outdoor adventure that others only dream of.

By the time you finish reading this book, it is my sincere hope that you will be "hooked on Baja" every bit as much as I am.

The Two Coasts

My love affair with the Baja California peninsula began more than five decades ago when my family used to go camping near the Punta Banda Estero south of Ensenada. After a day of fishing and swimming on a sun-drenched beach, I would reluctantly slip into my sleeping bag and allow myself to be lulled to sleep under blanket of stars by the sounds of the pounding surf and the changing of the tides at the mouth of the sandy inlet.

In those days, the scenic toll highway that now exists had not yet been built, and the old road to Ensenada turned abruptly inland just past the small poblado of Alisitos. Beyond that point, the southern coast was practically inaccessible to normal passenger vehicles. The rocky gravel road was narrow and punctuated by numerous, axle-busting dips and washboard-textured offshoots, some which led to a dead end of cactus and sagebrush, while others provided access to hidden turquoise coves filled with schools of hungry fish.

As a youth, I regularly pursued my catches from both above and below the surface of the water, and was comfortable using either a rod and reel or a Hawaiian sling spear. The first time I dipped into the water to explore one of these areas, I was mesmerized by the vast array of species before my eyes. Huge schools of sargo, also known as China croaker, weaved deftly in and out between strands of golden kelp, while closer to the bottom, big California sheephead weighing 15 pounds or more peeked out from under eelgrass-covered reefs.

From the sandy beaches nearby, we would cast into the surf using mussels and sand crabs for bait and catch nearly endless numbers of corbina and barred surfperch, many of which had managed to reach their maximum weight of about 3 pounds. On occasions when we would camp overnight, the day usually ended with a wonderful seafood feast of campfire-grilled fish fillets that was often teamed with fresh clams, mussels, octopus, and other delicacies that had been foraged from just beyond the adjacent shoreline.

We were, without a doubt, hooked on Baja.

Although factors such as commercial development and an ongoing influx of population may have superficially changed its face, those seeking an easily accessible angling adventure within a few hundred miles of the United States–Mexico border still need look no further than the shores of Baja California Norte.

Northern Baja (Baja California Norte)

Today, the Pacific coast of northern Baja offers a chance to catch limits from a long list of deepwater fish during the cooler months of the year. Many hardcore "rock codders" from the United States now migrate south during winter in pursuit of such table-friendly species as lingcod, rock cod, and other members of the genus *Sebastes,* which fall under strict catch moratoriums in southern California during the same time of year.

As the water begins to warm, northern Baja's inshore surface bite gets into full swing, and schools of exotic pelagic species such as yellowfin tuna and dorado can often be found around scattered, northbound kelp paddies drifting just offshore.

Albacore tuna have historically been one of the most popular pelagic species to visit the Pacific waters of Baja Norte during the summertime, although that predisposition has been negatively affected during the recent El Niño cycles. Sushi and sashimi lovers may prefer yellowfin or bluefin tuna, but the albacore remains one of the most highly prized members of the family. Their tasty white flesh has earned it the well-known moniker of "chicken of the sea," and it also happens to be the only species of tuna that can legally be labeled as "white meat." Whether you choose to cook, smoke, or can them, fillets of freshly caught Baja albacore are a gourmet delicacy.

Nonetheless, despite the often fevered offshore action, one of my favorite summertime pursuits is leisurely drifting near inshore kelp beds in pursuit of seasonal favorites such as calico bass, yellowtail, bonito, and large California barracuda, which often feed near surface bait schools and can be taken using live bait, plastic jigs, and surface iron.

One of the most convenient ways to reach Baja Norte is by

automobile. On the Pacific side, the scenic toll road linking Tijuana with Ensenada allows you excellent access to numerous breathtaking views of the Pacific Ocean, as well as an occasional line of pelicans gliding casually a few feet above the water's surface. The highway is well maintained, and far safer to navigate when pulling a boat and trailer than is the free road that runs nearby.

Just south of Tijuana, Rosarito Beach was once one of my favorite shore fishing destinations, but has since turned into a town that is visited mostly by tourists and partiers. To the west, the inshore waters between nearby Islas Los Coronados south to Ensenada's Bahía de Todos Santos comprise Baja Norte's legendary "Halibut Triangle."

Those who take advantage of the opportunity to drag a live mackerel along the bottom while making summertime drifts over one of the many sandy areas in this region stand a good chance of landing the halibut of their dreams. Although this type of fishing is usually feast or famine, catching flatties in the 20- to 40-pound class along this section of coast is not uncommon. The closest boat access is at Puerta la Salina, a few miles down the highway from the famed lobster village of Puerto Nuevo.

The Hotel Coral features an upscale marina that lies just north of Ensenada's commercial harbor. It is an excellent departure point for

The Hotel Coral's state-of-the-art marina at the northern end of Ensenada's Bahía de Todos Santos offers an excellent starting point for a fishing adventure in northern Baja. (LYNN GATCH)

vessels headed out on either short- or long-range voyages. Although far from inexpensive, the price of launching your boat at this facility also includes access to a washdown area, fish-cleaning station and hot showers, all of which are valuable amenities after an active day on the water.

Summer is the best time in this region to catch albacore (also called longfin tuna), one of the most sought-after members of the tuna family, as well as other popular gamesters including yellowtail, calico bass, bonito, and barracuda. During years when the water is warmer, dorado (also called dolphin or mahi-mahi) and yellowfin, bluefin, and bigeye tuna often join the fray.

Islas de Todos Santos, just offshore from Ensenada, offers productive fishing near the lee side drop-offs and world-class surfing on huge winter-time waves from the beaches on the west-facing shoreline. (LYNN GATCH)

For those without the benefit of having their own craft, there are numerous local charter boats and sport fishing services near the city's main malecon that are available to take anglers on half-day, three-quarter-day, or full-day fishing trips in the outer bay, around nearby Islas Todos Santos, or to points beyond.

Excellent summertime fishing is also on tap for anglers who charter a boat and guide from any of the three more southerly panga camps located at Punta Banda, Puerto Santo Tomás, or Castro's Camp in Erendira. These types of trips usually visit areas that are more remote, and generally yield more prolific and varied catches than many of the larger, commercial sportfishers in the area.

Fishing from beach-launched pangas is a common practice on both sides of the Baja coast. (LYNN GATCH)

Farther down the coast, Bahía San Quintin is the southernmost area in Baja Norte's Pacific coast that offers a conventional launch ramp and commercial sport fishing services. Just like other locations to the north, the summer months here can occasionally bring in migrating schools of

The ramp next to Bahía San Quintin's Old Mill and nearby restaurant is the primary launching facility in the region. (LYNN GATCH)

Capt. Kelly Catian (left) and client, Randy Peters, hoist a huge San Quintin white sea bass. (K&M SPORTFISHING)

yellowfin tuna and dorado to join large yellowtail and white sea bass to delight the many anglers who visit the area from Southern California and points beyond.

Inshore, the waters surrounding nearby San Martin Island can hold extremely prolific populations of a vast array of species, including big white sea bass over 50 pounds and tasty bottom dwellers such as lingcod and red rock cod. Lodging, restaurants, fishing charters, and launching facilities are readily available at the northern end of the bay.

Several miles south of San Quintin, the Transpeninsular Highway turns abruptly inland at the small town of El Rosario, which is about 230 miles below the international border, and then stretches east across the center of the peninsula toward the Sea of Cortez before heading south once again. The botanical curiosities along this stretch of highway combine to provide a unique and surreal landscape for travelers who have never before seen the peculiar, curling appendages of a cirio tree, the stately, humanlike stature of a giant cardón cactus, or the gray, thickly gnarled trunk of an elephant tree.

About 70 miles down the road, the small poblado of Cataviña offers motorists one of their last opportunities to top off their gas tanks or check into a motel room before passing through a region that is virtually bereft of such travelers' facilities. It is also home to historic

A wide variety of eerily unusual flora and fauna greets drivers heading south from El Rosaria. (MARIE-PIERRE)

Rancho Santa Ynez, a longtime oasis in a parched region that has one of the lowest annual rainfalls on earth.

Thirty-five miles or so south of Cataviña, a turnoff on the left over the dry lake bed of Laguna Chapala is the first tributary past Ensenada to provide access to the Sea of Cortez. It is simply graded and subject to all the deteriorative factors that affect most of Baja's backroads, particularly the washboard effect that provides a free—often unwanted—massage to drivers and passengers inside vehicles that are traveling faster than 10 to 15 miles per hour. Nonetheless, this somewhat primitive corridor offers a viable alternate approach to reaching rural coastal venues such as Punta Final, Bahía Gonzaga, and Puertecitos. These are areas that are also visited by motorists who approach the area via the northeasterly route, along Mexico's Highway 5, which connects San Felipe with the border city of Mexicali.

Beyond Laguna Chapala, the Punta Prieta turnoff is situated 30 miles farther down Mexico's Highway 1. It connects the main highway with the island-festooned angler's paradise of Bahía de Los Angeles, a region that also includes Bahía de las Animas and Bahía San Francisquito. We will take a closer look at this section of Baja Norte's Sea of Cortez coast between San Felipe and Bahía de Los Angeles later in the chapter.

A little more than 40 miles south of the Punta Prieta road to the east, the westbound Punta Rosarito turnoff offers motorists their first chance to reach the Pacific Ocean after passing through El Rosario just south of Bahía San Quintin. This area is popular with dedicated shore anglers, avid surfers, and those who enjoy a primitive camping experience, but it is also a bit tricky to reach in standard passenger vehicles, particularly if you are a first-timer.

The same is true for Morro Santo Domingo, which can be reached by taking the Jesus Maria turnoff about 20 miles farther south. After arriving at the coast, the graded trail heading north provides a pathway to many beaches and coves that offer very good fishing for yellowfin and spotfin croaker, corbina, and even big halibut on a few of the sandy-bottom spots. Please be aware, however, that *all* of Baja's secluded, off-road areas should be considered potentially dangerous, and possibly even deadly, unless extreme care, common sense, and the proper safety precautions are faithfully exercised. Bandits, though less common than in the past, can still be a threat, especially for parties of fewer than six people.

Southern Baja (Baja California Sur)

South of the border 445 miles, you will encounter the turnoff for the town of Guerrero Negro adjacent to Bahía Vizcaíno, which is named for Spanish explorer Sebastián Vizcaíno (1548–1624), and lies inside the giant "hook" near the middle of Baja's western coast.

This town also marks the border between the two estados of Baja California Norte and Baja California Sur. Visitors will find modest restaurants and accommodations here, as well as the usual tourist services. Guerrero Negro's primary enterprise, however, is providing dehydration facilities for raw sea salt, which is eventually taken just offshore to Cedros Island for processing prior to being transported to commercial buyers worldwide.

Immediately south of town, the popular Scammons Lagoon is the northernmost destination on the Baja coast for the migrating gray whales that visit here each year to birth their young. For anglers, the region marks a transition point in more ways than one. The Pacific Ocean waters south of here are subject to more tropical influences, and harbor many more exotic species of fish and other marine life that becomes far more prolific the farther south you proceed. While Guerrero Negro itself may not be a particularly enticing fishing destination, a few places immediately to the south definitely are.

The Vizcaíno turnoff is less than 50 miles south of the Guerrero Negro exit, and offers access to a popular venue for kayak and cartop boat anglers. At the farthest extremity, Bahía Tortugas provides an exceptional opportunity to catch quality calico bass, as well as bonito, barracuda, yellowtail, and even halibut. This small poblado is located next to Puerto San Bartolome, which offers a small launch ramp as well as a fuel dock for both commercial and recreational vessels.

Just down the coast, the bucolic Bahía Asunción features an even more secluded fishing venue for catching many of the same species. But if you plan to visit either of these spots, you should also make sure that you are well supplied with gasoline, water, and other vital provisions; Bahía Tortugas is located more than 100 miles, and Bahía Asunción more than 70 miles, from the Transpeninsular Highway. A majority of this distance traverses graded, washboard-surface roads, which can make progress rather slow. Just relax, take some time, and forget about the trailers and motor homes on this one.

Back on Mexico's Highway 1, approximately 30 miles below the offshoot to Bahía Tortugas and Bahía Asunción, the Abreojos turnoff leads to a stretch of coastline that features some of the very finest beach and shore fishing to be found anywhere on the Pacific coast. It is also a very productive area for anglers using kayaks and small boats.

About 45 miles southwest of the exit, you will encounter another graded road that leads off to the left and allows access to Estero de Coyote and Campo Rene, which has the only angler-oriented accommodations in the area, though they are Spartan. There is a modest launch ramp and limited supplies, along with an abbreviated landing strip for small private aircraft. If you bypass that turn and continue southwest, Punta Abreojos is only 7 miles farther down the road. This small poblado is dedicated to the harvesting and processing of seafood products, and is accordingly laid back in its demeanor. From there, the graded passage leading north eventually meets La Bocana, which is at the mouth of a small lagoon that shares the same name.

Due to excessive gillnetting by local commercial fishing cooperatives, the various gamefish species are not as prolific in these intertidal zones as they once were, though they still offer great fishing opportunities for the kayaker and cartop boater. The spotted bay bass is perhaps the most dependable target, with a fish weighing 3 pounds or more being fairly common. Depending upon the season, there can also be excellent fishing for halibut, shortfin corvina, and occasional grouper in the esteros as well.

The surf zone is this area is not as heavily netted, and provides awesome action for fat corbina, halibut, and white sea bass from spring through fall. Just off the coast, the rocky Abreojos reefs provide a perfect habitat for a variety of much larger fish in the tropical sea bass family, such as big cabrilla, baquetta, and a variety of other groupers.

Once back on Highway 1, you're only 10 miles from the intersection to reach the town of San Ignacio, as well as the famous San Ignacio Lagoon. To hopeful anglers surveying an oceanic chart, these waters may look extremely fishy and, in fact, they once were. Unfortunately, this and many other similar areas around Baja and the rest of the world have been severely impacted by the practice of inshore gillnetting.

In addition to commercial fishing pressure, the Mexican government's efforts to protect the calving California gray whales who regularly visit these waters have resulted in strict prohibitions on all but specially licensed boats and guides during the breeding season. But, while this may be a great place to get a close-up look at migrating whales, most veteran anglers who visit the region will agree that there are many other fishing areas nearby that better deserve your investment of time and gasoline.

South of here, the Transpeninsular Highway turns toward the southeast and eventually passes many popular fishing villages along the shoreline of the Sea of Cortez before meandering back toward the west coast again.

Approximately 50 miles past the exit for San Ignacio, you will encounter the historically noteworthy town of Santa Rosalia, which is also well respected as one of the prime fishing destinations along the Cortez coast of Baja California Sur. Before actually arriving there, however, you will come to a small side road that heads north for a little over 7 miles to a relatively tiny cove known as Caleta Santa Maria. For those with small cartop boats and kayaks, this out-of-the-way, semi-industrial venue offers good beach launching and excellent fishing most of the year for spotted bay bass, triggerfish, and occasional leopard grouper. During warmer months, the waters just outside the cove feature good surface action for sierra, skipjack, yellowtail, dorado, and sometimes even yellowfin tuna.

The architecture of Santa Rosalia, immediately to the south, pos-

Santa Rosalia's distinctive European-style architecture was brought by the French during the late 1800s. (MARIE-PIERRE)

sesses a distinctly French influence since, in 1885, a French company named El Boleo acquired rights to set up a copper mining facility there in exchange for building the town as well as an adjacent harbor and ferry system for transporting workers in from Guaymas, which lies just across the Gulf of California on the Mexican mainland.

Just south of Santa Rosalia lies the naturally protected San Lucas cove and nearby Isla San Marcos, just across Craig Channel. The inshore waters harbor spotted bay bass, cabrilla, and leopard grouper, while the channel allows access to seasonally exceptional fishing for yellowtail, dorado, yellowfin, and skipjack tuna as well as the ceviche-friendly sierra. Fishing around the island can also be very productive, especially near deep pinnacles and holes where big grouper and snapper wait within rocky lairs to ambush their prey and play havoc with the terminal tackle of the anglers who would pursue them.

About 15 miles farther down the main highway, the turnoff to Punta Chivato leads to an area that has become extremely popular with many seasoned Baja anglers over the years. Inshore, the spotted bay bass, which are extremely prolific to the north, is almost nonexistent here, but the leopard grouper becomes a far more common catch. To be perfectly honest, I've yet to meet a fisherman who has been saddened by this discovery, since a chunky leopard grouper grows many times larger than a spotted bay bass and makes far better table fare.

The waters between Punta Chivato and the southern end of San Marcos Island offer excellent opportunities for scuba divers and for anglers in pursuit of big gulf grouper and pargo. Two miles to the southeast, the small islands of Santa Ines provide great seasonal fishing for a variety of popular gamefish, including yellowfin tuna, dorado, sailfish, and marlin.

Just past Punta Chivato lies a longtime tourist destination, Mulegé, the palm-studded oasis that was established by Spanish missionaries centuries ago on the banks of one of Baja's few rivers, just a few miles upstream from the Sea of Cortez. Its dense groves of date palms still provide sweet, delicious fruit to augment the other prolific tropical produce that is grown commercially in the area. The huge bay south of town known as Bahía Conception was once a treasure trove of clams, scallops, and other shellfish. But sadly, the side effects of a constantly growing population and decades of overfishing have reduced its natural bounty to a mere fraction of what it once was.

Loreto, about 80 miles south of Mulegé, was once one of the primary destinations for angling enthusiasts during the early days of southern Baja's recreational sport fishing industry in the middle of the last century. Since then, many other areas have been developed to appeal to this market, but despite the popularity of Cabo San Lucas and

Mulegé is a true oasis in the middle of Baja's sizzling landscape.
(RICK ROESSLER)

East Cape fishing resorts, Loreto still holds its own when it comes to seasonally hot rod-bending action. It is also the last major township along Mexico's Highway 1 before it weaves its way back toward Baja Sur's Pacific coast.

Another 80 miles below Loreto, the Ciudad Insurgentes turnoff

Loreto offers palm-covered beaches as well as excellent fishing for a variety of popular species. (MARIE-PIERRE)

provides access to Bahía Magdalena, less than 40 miles to the south-west. This highly revered region has been a favorite of adventurous Baja anglers for decades, and offers a wide variety of offshore, inshore, and onshore fishing venues for a vast assortment of popular gamefish species. Over the past several years, the area has also become a magnet for a burgeoning number of ecotourists who augment the yearly influx of whale watchers who visit the area.

The California gray whale can generally be observed migrating south along the Baja coast between December and April, while smaller pods of these huge creatures are also visible from the coasts of British Columbia, Washington, Oregon, and California. Their prime breeding grounds are found within the warm waters of Magdalena Bay, as well as in San Ignacio Lagoon and Scammons Lagoon to the north.

In addition to hosting whale lovers, the port city of San Carlos inside the Bahía supports numerous tourist-oriented operations that cater to a diverse range of recreational tastes in practically every demographic group. The lagoon is a narrow channel protected from the open sea by Isla Magdalena. The abundant sand dunes on the island stand in stark contrast to the thick, impenetrably tangled growths of mangroves that flourish along its inner coast.

At the northern end of Santa Maria Bay the tricky access to Punta Hughes rewards determined surfers with some of the finest breaks on the local coast, while practically endless stretches of adjacent sandy beach make for unparalleled beachcombing opportunities.

Magdalena Bay is also home to several types of endangered sea turtles and many other commercially valuable fish and invertebrate species such as scallops, crabs, clams, and shrimp. Small poblados along its shore depend almost entirely upon fishing activities for their livelihood. Unfortunately, years of overharvesting, as well as the negative effects of the bycatch of commercial fishing, have proved to be highly detrimental to the bay's ability to regenerate its own native marine life. Incidents of juvenile loggerhead turtles being captured in halibut gillnets within the bay are still fairly common.

Back on the main road, the next major community heading south on the Baja highway is La Paz. Since its formal establishment in the late 1500s, this city has been a virtual magnet for missionaries, pearl divers, and pirates. The latter were said to have regularly anchored in the beautiful bay to re-supply and refurbish their vessels, as well as to lay claim to any and all valuables that came within their grasp during sometimes lengthy visits.

Images of the rocky southern tip of Baja California have been featured in everything from home videos to major motion pictures. (RICK ROESSLER)

Today, it is a thriving tourist center that, along with its spectacular scenery and many water-oriented activities, has also been named by *Money* magazine as the number one place in the world to retire.

Just over 130 miles south lies Cabo San Lucas, the well-known rocky point that marks the end of the Baja peninsula. There are two ways to reach this area from La Paz; one is simply by continuing south on the main highway.

The other option is the more leisurely and picturesque coastal route, which passes through Los Barriles and Baja Sur's legendary angler's paradise known as the East Cape.

Once in the Los Cabos region, visitors have a choice between the fast-moving, highly commercialized town of Cabo San Lucas, or its more laid-back neighbor, San José del Cabo. No matter where you choose to hang your hat, however, you can count on having a wide assortment of upscale hotels, resorts, and restaurants eagerly awaiting your arrival. But because this is a very popular area, travelers should always make sure that they have made arrangements for lodging prior to their arrival, particularly in the peak of tourist season.

San Felipe to Bahía de Los Angeles

The eastern coast of Baja Norte is situated on the Sea of Cortez and supports an entirely different type of habitat and fishery than the Pacific side. Volcanic outcroppings and occasional groups of small, rugged islands intermittently interrupt the miles of warm, sandy beach that adjoin this tepid desert sea.

South of San Felipe, the narrow highway heading toward Puertecitos, 50 miles away, runs parallel to long stretches of unpopulated sand beach that are a kayak angler's dream. Catches of large orange-mouth corvina are not uncommon here during summer. Puertecitos offers a small launch ramp and limited facilities and is not far from Las Islas Encantadas, which are known for excellent summertime fishing for white sea bass, yellowtail, and leopard grouper.

The dusty, uneven thoroughfare south of Puertecitos has a long-standing reputation as one of the most rutted roads in northern Baja. It can be very intimidating, and probably should not be undertaken except by the most seasoned of Baja travelers. That said, the secluded areas of Bahía Willard and Bahía Gonzaga several miles down the coast are not only breathtakingly beautiful, but also offer great on-shore, inshore, and offshore angling opportunities throughout the entire summer.

Bahía de Los Angeles is a very popular fishing location that lies even further south, but is best reached by automobile via the Transpeninsular Highway. As is true along the entire Cortez coast, summer visitors to "L.A. Bay" should expect extremely warm daytime temperatures and plenty of sunshine. There is now a new hotel located next to the main panga fishing operation, a launch ramp, and several places in the area to camp. During the summertime, nearby islands attract large schools of baitfish as well as big white sea bass, yellowtail, skipjack, grouper, and cabrilla.

The region is also home to the world's largest cactus, the giant cardón, which can reach a height of over 60 feet. The first time I ever saw one of these huge cacti, I mistakenly referred to it as a saguaro. This is a common mix-up, since it greatly resembles a smaller, related species that is common in the deserts of Arizona. Native Americans believed that the cardón cactus could actually take on human attributes and move around the desert at night while they were asleep.

There are a number of other specimens dotting this arid landscape, such as the notorious and occasionally painful cholla, also known as "jumping cactus." Also present are a plethora of barrel cacti, pitahaya, and nopal, which produces bright red fruit rich in precious moisture.

The roots, leaves, seeds, and fruits of many of these native plants provided a valuable source of food and water for the indigenous people, who survived for thousands of years in this harsh ecosystem before the first Europeans ever set foot here.

Young, tender nopal leaves, pitahaya, and cactus fruit are still relished in northern Baja California today.

One thing is certain; however you get there, wherever you go, there is a special magic that exists in this section of Baja Norte's desert that consistently manages to enchant visitors, many of whom never suspected that they would eventually fall under its spell.

The Fish of Baja

A Note About Catch-and-Release

There are well over a thousand species of fish that swim in the waters around the Baja peninsula. The ones listed here are those most commonly targeted by anglers. Throughout this book you will find continuing references to the culinary preparation of various fish species. For many, this is very important information since fish remains a prime protein food source for billions of people around the world. On the other hand, scientific data also shows us that fish stocks are now being depleted to perilously low levels. While some may ascribe much of this problem to commercial fishing interests, there is no doubt that "overlimit" fishing and unadulterated waste by thoughtless recreational anglers plays a significant role as well. May all those who read this book with the desire and intent to keep and eat their catch faithfully remember to keep *only* what they can actually preserve and consume. The fishing success of future generations depends upon our vigilance today.

Striped Marlin (*Tetrapturus audax*)

Most striped marlin taken in Baja inhabit the waters of Baja Sur, particularly off Los Cabos and the East Cape throughout much of the year. But striped marlin can also be successfully targeted off the Pacific coast of Baja Norte during summer, when they and a bevy of other migrating pelagic gamefish make there way up the Baja coast to briefly visit the seas off of the coastal islands in northern Baja and southern California.

In past decades, trolling was the most common method for finding and catching marlin, particularly when they are observed meandering

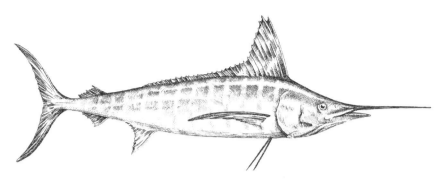

Striped marlin (SCOTT KENNEDY)

around near the surface. On other occasions, lures are trolled through an area in an attempt to provoke a blind strike. Live bait also works well, but it requires a lot more effort, since the fish must be visually located and then cast to.

Recently, however, the popularity of fly fishing for marlin has skyrocketed. The flies used for taking marlin are usually 12 to 14 inches long, and come in various patterns that have been crafted to represent baits such as squid, mackerel, and small bonito. Don't get me wrong, marlin will attack much smaller flies than that, but their hooks are almost always far too small for the really big guys.

Nonetheless, trolling is still one of the best ways to find marlin that you can't see, but it is always a good idea not to be fishing alone when you intend to go after one. An especially exciting moment for a friend of mine who did not heed this advice came when he was by himself casually trolling for dorado offshore just southwest of San Diego, and adjacent to the international boundary with Mexican waters.

During his lone quest to find a quality dorado or yellowfin tuna, he decided to troll a pink Zuker jethead lure behind his boat, but little did he know that it would be suddenly inhaled by a roving striped marlin. After a 40-minute battle, both he and the fish were totally exhausted as he grabbed the short leader.

It was apparent that the great fish would not survive their heated battle, so he was eventually able to shove his hand and forearm up under the marlin's gill plate and, after much frustrating effort, manage to wrestle the huge fish onto his deck. This placed him in rather unique company, since only a handful of highly skilled anglers have ever performed an amazing feat of this nature. Back at the dock in San Diego, his striped marlin weighed out at just over 110 pounds.

Although his experience makes for a great fish story, I still would not recommend that anyone go after marlin single-handedly.

Yellowfin Tuna (*Thunnus albacares*)

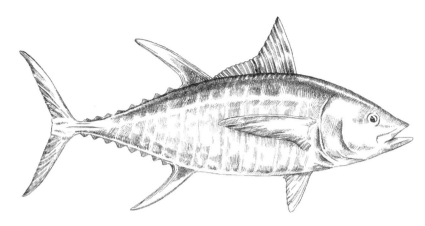

Yellowfin tuna (SCOTT KENNEDY)

Yellowfin tuna are the most commonly caught tuna species in Baja. This is not to say that anglers do not actively target albacore, bluefin, and bigeye tuna as well—it's simply that the yellowfin is the most prevalent tuna overall.

Though the chickenlike white meat of the albacore, and the precious loin of the bluefin tuna—known as maguro in sushi bars—may rank a bit higher on the preference list of seafood gourmets, the tasty

Yellowfin tuna come in many sizes, from 12-pound footballs like this one caught on a fly rod, to 200-pound "cows." (JEFF DEBROWN)

yellowfin can still hold its own. It is a big favorite both on the grill and in restaurants, where it is often referred to by its Hawaiian name, ahi.

Yellowfin tuna come in all sizes. They range from the small, football-shaped fish in the 6- to 10-pound class caught early in the season off Baja Sur—and in late summer and fall along the Pacific coast of Baja Norte—to the 300-pound giants targeted by San Diego's long-range sport fishing fleet.

Yellowfin are most easily located under working birds, which are also attacking the schools of frenzied baitfish that the tuna and other gamefish have pushed up from the depths. Trolling hard baits, daisy chains, spreader bars, and jethead skirts at speeds between 7 and 9 knots is an effective method of locating large, solitary rogues as well as school-sized yellowfin. Once on the fish, chumming is one of the best ways to keep them around the boat so that they can then be caught using live bait, a lure, or a fly.

Albacore (*Thunnus alalunga*)

Albacore (SCOTT KENNEDY)

The albacore, or longfin, is a particularly popular member of the tuna family and is found in temperate seas around the world. In the eastern Pacific they range from south of Guadalupe Island, Baja California, north to southeast Alaska. The albacore's diet varies greatly, depending upon where they happen to be feeding in the water column and what is available to them.

Most albacore fishing takes place between 20 and 100 miles from shore. Studies by marine scientists indicate that 57 of every 100 albacore caught are hooked in water ranging in temperature between 60 and 64 degrees Fahrenheit. As the season progresses, even more longfins will continue migrating into Baja waters. By late August, a throng of other pelagic species, such as dorado and yellowfin tuna, also join them.

After catching your first albacore of the day, it is always a smart idea to check out its stomach contents to discover the types of organisms that it has been feeding on recently. This information will often assist you in figuring out what kind of bait or lure to use to increase your catch. Another good way to find out what the albacore are eating is to arrive at the fishing grounds well before dawn and turn on the deck lights to ascertain what kind of forage ends up being attracted to the boat.

Having the proper tackle is an absolute must when targeting any member of the tuna family. Rods should generally be 6 to 7 feet in length with relatively pliable tips. Always select a sturdy, conventional-style reel with a star or lever drag system that is packed with high-quality 25- to 40-pound-test monofilament line. Attempting to go after albacore with even the heaviest spinning gear is a tactical error.

Selecting the correct hook size is also important. Anchovies usually require a small, No. 2 or No. 4 live bait hook that won't kill them, while big sardines will often take a No. 1/0 or No. 2/0 hook. For best results, always try to match the size of your hook to the size of your bait. While most albacore are taken on live baitfish such as anchovies or sardines, trolling with feathers or other lures near working birds or surface disturbances is another way to find longfins when they are in any given area.

It is also crucial to monitor the ocean surface temperature closely to determine where the current breaks are, then troll on the warmest side using hard baits or feather jigs. In the past few years, anglers have rediscovered the plain cedar plug, which was widely used along the Pacific coast during the 1940s and 1950s. Ironically, although they are now available in most of the same modern colors as trolling feathers, the plain wood finish continues to provoke more fish to strike than other hues. On some days, the longfins may show a decided partiality for cedar plugs over any other lure in your tackle box.

Try trolling at speeds between 6.5 and 7.5 knots. When one of your rigs gets hit, try to carefully circle the school while leaving the hooked fish in the water well behind the transom. More albacore can then be taken using either live bait or plastic swimbaits, which are more effective in reaching the larger fish that tend to swim near the bottom of the school. Cast the swimbait as far upcurrent as possible, let it sink

Gene Coombs and "Baja Bev" Seltzer show off their freshly caught "chicken of the sea." (BEVERLY SELTZER)

between 20 and 100 feet, then bring the lure in with a medium to fast retrieve.

Whether you pursue albacore by trolling or bait fishing, there is one relatively new tool on the market that will definitely enhance your success. The recent advent of fluorocarbon fishing line has revolutionized the sport fishing industry. Fluorocarbon is virtually invisible in the water, and using it to make a 6- to 8-foot leader is one of the most effective ways to increase your number of strikes and hook-ups. Fluorocarbon also has incredible abrasion resistance and higher sensitivity, and offers superior knot strength compared to nylon monofilament.

When an albacore bite is wide open, it is easy to get caught up in the frenzy of the action and try to catch as many fish as possible. While this is perfectly permissible in United States waters, where there is no daily limit on longfins, an equivalent policy does not exist in the Republic of Mexico. In the waters off Baja California, albacore are subject to exactly the same take limits as any other saltwater gamefish.

This may well be a more intelligent strategy than the one practiced north of the border, since we now possess a scientific understanding that no natural resource is truly inexhaustible.

While boats out of southern California are now traveling 40 to 100 miles offshore to find albacore, sport fishers based in Ensenada have been able to catch them much closer to port, which has even allowed a few ¾-day boats to occasionally take albacore. Now that major marinas, like the one at Hotel Coral, are in full operation, there is little excuse for private boaters not to trailer their craft a few hours south on the well-maintained toll highway to take advantage of the action.

After the fishing is done, the catch has been cleaned, and the barbecue has been lit, fresh albacore fillets become a gourmet delicacy when lightly marinated in Italian dressing and grilled over glowing mesquite coals. Sushi and sashimi lovers may prefer yellowfin or bluefin tuna, but the albacore remains one of the most highly prized members of the tuna family. Their rich, tasty flesh has earned them the well-known moniker "chicken of the sea," and albacore are the only species of tuna that can legally be labeled as "white meat." Whether you choose to cook, smoke, or can your catch, bleeding out and icing down your freshly caught tuna will make an incredible difference in the ultimate flavor and quality of your final product.

Dorado (*Coryphaena hippurus*)

Dorado (SCOTT KENNEDY)

The dorado is truly one of the golden treasures of saltwater sport fishing. Referred to as mahi-mahi in Hawaii and dolphinfish in the southeastern United States, it is one of the fastest-growing fish species in the ocean, and packs on an additional 10 pounds every year that it is alive.

Those who are familiar with the fishing in Cabo San Lucas and the East Cape know that dorado are an important staple of that region's sport fishing industry during the warmer months. They are prolific, colorful, and absolutely delectable as table fare.

Dorado often congregate under floating debris such as flotsam, Sargasso grass, and—in the waters of northern Baja—beneath selected kelp paddies found drifting offshore during late summer. Recently, anglers fishing off the coast between San Quintin and the border have been running into a few dorado that have tipped the scale at over 30 pounds. When brought aboard, the dorado flashes brilliantly with vibrant hues of gold, green, and blue. Unfortunately, these beautiful colors are short-lived after the fish expires.

Dorado are not particularly picky eaters, and will generally take just about any kind of offering when they are hungry. Large bulls, sometimes over 40 pounds, can also be incidentally hooked later in the season by anglers trolling for marlin. Dorado have a reputation for making a series of spectacular leaps after the initial hook-up. If your fish decides to jump, it is extremely important to remember to keep your rod tip high and take up any slack in the line, since this is when most dorado are lost after spitting the hook.

Want to catch more dorado? One of the best tricks is to leave a hooked fish in the water, and then have fellow anglers toss baits or lures nearby. Dorado are very curious, and other fish in the school will often move in close to see what is going on. This is when multiple hook-ups are likely to take place. After awhile, the fish may spook and go deep, but if you mark your GPS waypoint, you can always return to the same spot later in the day when there may be more dorado waiting to be caught.

Fresh dorado is delicious prepared in a number of ways. One of the quickest and most popular methods is to simply grill it over glowing mesquite coals. When using this technique, try first marinating the boneless fillets in a mixture of one small can of frozen orange juice concentrate and ½ cup of brown sugar. This will create a toothsome, almost "sweet-and-sour"-type glaze that pairs perfectly with the delicate flavor and texture of the fish.

There is also the Hawaiian cooking method, which involves lightly dredging the fillets in seasoned flour, beaten egg, and crushed macadamia nuts. After quickly pan searing on both sides, and finishing in a 450-degree oven for about seven to ten minutes, you can enjoy a sumptuous repast that would be fit for King Kamehameha.

Yellowtail (*Seriola lalandi*)

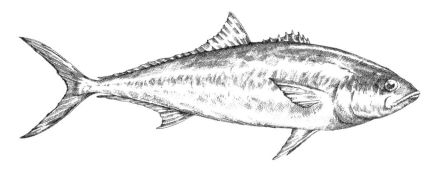

Yellowtail (SCOTT KENNEDY)

Yellowtail, the gamefish that made Ensenada famous, is one of the most sought-after species throughout Baja California. Fortunately, they can be caught somewhere around the peninsula at practically any time of year.

Fishing for yellowtail is generally good in the spring and fall, but usually reaches its peak during summer. These fish are usually found between 5 and 60 miles offshore, and can be located electronically near offshore banks, islands, or kelp paddies. The traditional method involves looking for surface disturbances that draw groups of circling and diving birds. You may also find success by fishing on the warmwater side of offshore temperature breaks.

When yellowtail are on a surface bite, it's hard for them to turn down a properly presented live anchovy, sardine, or small mackerel. The best method is to live-line the bait on a weightless line. Match the size of your hook to the size of the bait you are using, and place it through the fish's nose in order to make it stay near the surface. If the school seems a little deeper, add a few split-shot or a small egg sinker to let the bait sink slightly as it swims away from the boat. To incite baits to swim deeper without the aid of added weight, hook anchovies near the collar, and sardines and mackerel near the anal opening. The best artificial bait to use in this situation is lighter surface iron in blue and white, blue and chrome, or scrambled egg colors.

Yellowtail can also be found at depths down to several hundred feet. These are the times when heavy iron jigs in green and yellow, scrambled egg, blue and chrome, or blue and white work best. Allow the iron to free-fall to the bottom, and retrieve at a medium to fast speed with a yo-yo action. Expect the bite to occur on the drop, but you can also get slammed on a quick retrieve up from the bottom. Yellowtail is one species that requires heavier tackle, such as 25- to 50-pound line on a standard conventional reel, as opposed to lightweight spinning gear.

As table fare, yellowtail tends to have a somewhat gamy flavor. Some may enjoy it as sashimi or when the fillets have been cooked over glowing coals, but I personally find it most toothsome after it has been smoked.

White Sea Bass (*Atractoscion nobilis*)

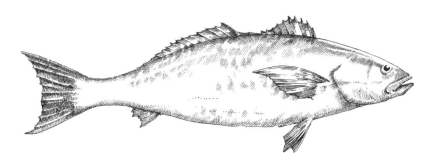

White sea bass (SCOTT KENNEDY)

The months between spring and fall in Baja Norte offer a window of time that can be extremely productive for those pursuing one of the most popular gamefish on both the Pacific and Cortez coasts, the white sea bass.

This prized gamefish, whose Latin name was recently changed from *Cynoscion nobilis* to *Atractoscion nobilis,* is not a true bass at all, but actually the largest member of the croaker family on the Pacific coast. It is second in size only to the giant, protected totuava in the northern Sea of Cortez. These fish range from Alaska to southern Baja, but are most common south of Point Conception.

Live squid are probably the best all-around bait for catching sea bass, but large anchovies and sardines are also effective. At times, larger specimens are more likely to bite on a live Pacific mackerel. This bait can be particularly deadly when trolled slowly near the inner edges of kelp beds during the predawn hours.

Seafood lovers consider the fresh fillets of white sea bass to be a gourmet delicacy, which can be prepared in a number of delicious ways. One quick and simple technique is to slather a thick chunk of sea bass in melted garlic butter and toss it onto a hot, smoky mesquite grill for several minutes. Baste the uncooked top once more, then turn and baste again until the fish flakes when probed with a fork. Finish off with a squeeze of lemon or lime, and get ready for a little bite of heaven.

White sea bass are fished primarily with live bait in relatively shallow water, but they will also take a fast-trolled spoon, artificial squid, or bone jig. White is one of the most effective colors for these fish. Live squid are considered one of the best baits for white sea bass, but large anchovies and medium-size sardines are also good. At times, large white sea bass will bite only on fairly large, live Pacific mackerel.

White sea bass can be caught along Baja's Pacific coast from Islas Los Coronados to points south past Bahía Magdalena. Along the northern Cortez coast, white sea bass are found from San Felipe to beyond San Francisquito.

Vermilion Rockfish (*Sebastes miniatus*)

Vermilion rockfish (SCOTT KENNEDY)

There are more than 20 members of the genus *Sebastes*, commonly called rockfish or rockcod, which generally reside in the deeper waters along Baja Norte's Pacific coast. Rockfishes are available year-round, and are excellent table fare. One of the most prized and targeted of these is the vermilion rockfish, commonly referred to as Pacific red snapper. The body of this species is somewhat husky and compressed. Its color is a brilliant orange red on the body and fins, and it may also exhibit a subtle black and gray mottling. Most *Sebastes* species are caught along Baja's Pacific coast between Islas Los Coronados near the international border and San Martin Island off Bahía San Quintin.

When coastal water temperatures begin to take their seasonal dip

A smiling John Sheppard with the first of his many vermilion rockfish caught along the coast of Baja Norte. (TOM GATCH)

during the winter months, most of the exotic species such as tuna will have already left the region. Anglers here would be in pretty bad shape as far as offshore fishing goes if it weren't for the excellent bottom fishing along Baja Norte's Pacific coast.

Vermilion rockfish can be taken with standard dropper loop rigs, several ounces of weight at the terminal end, and one or two hooks up the line a distance of 12 to 16 inches from each other. A good hole can often yield several species on any given day. Smaller rockfish are usually found in the same areas as larger members of the family. They will readily take anchovies and sardines, but it is often advisable to use a tough, difficult-to-steal bait such as squid or cut, sun-dried mackerel. Rockfish will also readily attack chrome-plated, pink, or white metal jigs enhanced by a strip of squid pinned to the hook.

Once cleaned and prepared for cooking, the rockfish displays perhaps its finest qualities. Rockfish fillets are delicious sautéed, baked, tempura-style, poached in white wine, or served *al mojo de ajo* in a garlic butter sauce—and they also make exceptional fish and chips. As far as quality and versatility goes, they may be second only to members of the true snapper family, *Lutjanidae,* when it comes to adaptability in the kitchen.

Lingcod (*Ophiodon elongates*)

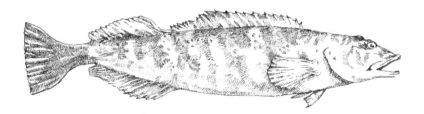

Lingcod (SCOTT KENNEDY)

Lingcod occur most abundantly at depths ranging around 350 feet, but will often go into even deeper water. A few have been caught as deep as 2,700 feet! Spawning occurs in January and February, when the females lay 150,000 to 500,000 eggs, then leave immediately. The males then take up the role of guardian. Adult lingcod prey on a variety of fish and have been known to be cannibalistic.

"Toothy, tenacious, and tasty" is a perfect description of the lingcod.

Contrary to popular belief, this fish is neither a "ling" nor a "cod," but actually a large member of the greenling family that is found between Punta San Carlos in Baja California, and Kodiak Island, Alaska. They are not abundant south of California's Point Conception except in a few localities, one of those being within the crisp waters of the Japanese Current, which cuts along the Pacific coast of northern Baja California.

Young lingcod feed primarily on shrimp and other small crustaceans until they are big enough to ambush live fish. Nearly all these fish reach maturity by four years of age, when they usually measure 26 inches or more. Lingcod are easily caught on conventional bottom rigs using anchovies, cut squid, or chunks of mackerel. Live bait is generally more successful than dead bait, and dead bait is often more effective than metal jigs.

That said, it is nonetheless true that some of the largest lingcod ever taken have ended up being caught on large, chrome-plated jigs once referred to as "bottom bouncers." One of my personal favorites is the jointed metal Action Lure, which can jiggle more enticingly in extremely deep water than standard "bottom iron." One suggestion when using heavy lures to target lingcod is to tip the hook with a small, whole squid and then drop it all the way to the bottom. Rapidly reel up 10 to 12 cranks, disengage the reel spool, and drop the jig back to the bottom again. Repeat this process several times as you drift along over deep, rocky structure—you may be rewarded with a jarring strike, a fervent battle, and a delicious dinner!

Sometimes, using live bait is the best way to catch this species. I'll never forget an impromptu trip to Ensenada's Bahía de Todos Santos that I took with an old fishing buddy more than 25 years ago. He was trying out his new 19-foot fiberglass skiff, and we both had been itching to get our lines wet in Baja for several months prior to its purchase.

In those days, good nautical facilities around Ensenada were few and far between, so we ended up paying a few dollars to launch at a commercial ramp located in the middle of the industrial port district. Once out on the water, our thoughts turned to acquiring bait, and we noticed a sport fisher from Gordo's Landing pulling away from a small platform that was manned by a lone attendant. We approached the concession and greeted the gentleman with friendly demeanors and broad smiles, only to be abruptly rebuffed when he refused our offer of a $10 bill in exchange for some live anchovies with a brusque *"¡No! Estos son sólo para barcos comerciales."* He sold bait only to commercial boats.

We had never bargained on a major glitch of this nature, but before we had a chance to try to strike some sort of bargain, two local sport fishing boats loaded with passengers simultaneously descended upon the small netted podium. The attendant was obviously outgunned, so we quickly took advantage of the opportunity to do him a favor by jumping from our tethered craft and helping him transport net after net of the flailing baitfish to the crews waiting onboard. After the second boat was baited up and had pulled away, I turned to him and extended my hand, covered with fish scales, holding $10. "Por favor, amigo." I offered simply.

"Okay, gringo," he said in broken English with a knowing grin. "You guys earn your bait." He quickly palmed the crumpled bill, stuck it into the pocket of his tattered Levis, and then promptly filled our small tank with as many live anchovies as it could safely handle. We were finally on our way.

The only question remaining was "on our way" to where? This was my first time out in a boat in that region that wasn't being guided by a professional skipper or pangero, and it was years before the development of the kind of sophisticated fish-finding electronics that we enjoy these days. The only obvious objective was to try to find some sort of cover or structure that might hold fish. We headed a few miles out toward Todos Santos Islands and then turned south. It wasn't long before we were in sight of the myriad of guano-covered pinnacles that thrust up intermittently from the surface between the islands and the tip of the Punta Banda peninsula.

The closer we got, the more we could tell that there was a lot going on; the surface was exploding with activity as seagulls and pelicans dove down from above. We quickly slid up to the edge of the melee and began lobbing live-lined baits toward the action. Wham! We both hooked up immediately. Our excitement waned, however, as we brought a couple of frenzied mackerel back to the rail. "Jeeeeez! It's a friggin' mac attack!" my buddy proclaimed in disgust. I was likewise disappointed, but was also happy that the skunk had been taken off the boat on our first stop.

After a few more mackerel, we casually decided to clip on a few ounces of weight and see what was on the bottom, which turned out to be a wise choice. Not only were both our anchovies inhaled by something hungry within seconds of reaching the bottom, but these fish were obviously much bigger than the pound-and-a-half mackerel that we had been catching. After a spirited fight, we cranked up a couple of long, vicious, blue-green monsters from the turquoise depths. "Lingcod!" we exclaimed joyfully, practically in unison.

As the day progressed, my friend and I continued to catch lings between 4 and 8 pounds until we were practically ashamed of ourselves. With a cooler full of fresh lingcod, we headed happily back to port. Later that evening, a successful fishing trip turned into unadulterated delight at the dinner table as we enjoyed a magnificent meal of mild, flaky fish fillets that had been baked in lemon butter and garlic with a pinch of dried tarragon. Somehow, the boneless fillets of those big, nasty lingcod had been magically transformed into one of the tastiest fish dinners that we had eaten for a long time.

Sculpin (*Scorpaena guttata*)

Sculpin (SCOTT KENNEDY)

Anyone who has ever spent much time around tide pools along the California coast has probably noticed small members of the sculpin family darting quickly among limpets, barnacles, and sea anemones. Then they practically disappear when they sit motionless, their natural camouflage blending with the mottled rocks around them.

Most sculpin are found in Pacific Ocean waters, but there also happens to be an isolated population that occurs in the upper portion of the Sea of Cortez. They are caught over hard, rocky bottoms from just below the water's surface to depths of more than 600 feet, and occasionally over mud or sand. They range in color from dark orange brown to bright red, and rarely exceed 4 pounds in weight. Their diet includes mussels, small crabs, squid, octopus, and a variety of the small fish that share their territory. Sculpin will readily take a piece of squid, mussel, or anchovy that has been lowered to the bottom in one of the rocky areas that they are known to inhabit. Small plastic grubs in various colors are also very effective in catching sculpin, particularly when tipped with a thin strip of squid. At times, chumming with small pieces of squid, mussel, or sea urchin will also help attract them to the area.

The firm, white, delicately flavored fillets of the sculpin may be relatively small, but they are a delightful treat for the gourmet palate and can be prepared in a variety of ways. My favorite technique is to dust them lightly in flour, dip them quickly in beaten egg, and then roll them in panko-style Japanese bread crumbs. After letting them set up in the refrigerator for about 20 minutes, they are lightly fried until golden brown in a mixture of equal parts olive oil and garlic butter.

But, alas, nature usually has a counterbalance in store for those who would harvest and consume the tastiest of its seafood delights. In the case of the the sculpin, it's the painfully sharp—and poisonous—dorsal and pectoral fins.

While growing up, I had always heard horrible stories about what happened when unlucky anglers found themselves on the business end of a sculpin's dorsal fin, and when I actually witnessed the event in living color, you can be assured that it was not a pretty sight.

I was aboard an open party sport fishing boat out of Ensenada in late spring many years ago when an unwary 16-year old fisherman visiting from Arizona turned from the rail holding up one of these spike-finned toads by the lip as if it were some kind of freshwater bass and chirped, "What the heck kind of fish is this ugly sucker?"

"Watch out, amigo!" shouted a nearby deckhand who immediately realized the peril that his young passenger was in. "Just drop the fish on the deck, my friend, I'll take care . . ." But it was too late.

"*Yeowwww!*" shrieked the unfortunate young man. "He *stuck* me! Oh, man . . . this really hurts!" He screamed as we all looked on, stunned and frozen by the unexpected turn of events. Within five minutes, he was lying on a bench inside the galley writhing in indescribable agony, his hand swollen to nearly twice its normal size. Our trip was justifiably cut short—the boat immediately headed back to port so that the passenger could receive much needed medical attention.

This word to the wise should be sufficient to remind everyone that the sculpin may be beguiling as table fare, but it must also be afforded the same respect that you would extend to a scorpion or a rattlesnake.

Kelp (calico) Bass (*Paralabrax clathratus*)

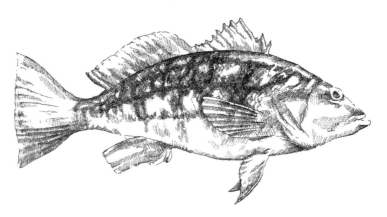

Kelp bass (SCOTT KENNEDY)

This colorful, checkerboard-patterned fish is a member of the family *Serranidae* (sea basses), and is also a close relative to spotted bay bass and barred sand bass.

The inshore region along Baja's northern Pacific coast is fortunate to be blessed with numerous concentrations of kelp, home to calico bass, one of the region's most prized gamefish. Members of this species will viciously attack a well-presented live anchovy, sardine, or lure, and have a reputation for hiding behind the cover of kelp strands so that they can lie in wait for unsuspecting prey as it swims by.

The calico bass is a prime target of coastal anglers because of its great fighting spirit, as well as for the quality table fare that it provides. Although most likely to weigh between 1 to 4 pounds, these fish can occasionally reach a weight of 12 or 13 pounds when living in their natural kelp bed habitat.

In addition to the kelp, calico bass also inhabit areas near shallow reefs, breakwaters, or "boiler" rocks, as well as just about any other inshore spot with submerged structure. They are also occasionally found in bays and harbors adjacent to docks and moorings, which provide suitable shelter from which they can ambush baitfish.

These popular gamesters will readily inhale most live forage species, particularly anchovies, sardines, smelt, and herring. They are also extremely fond of smaller live squid, although this bait is rather difficult to obtain predictably. Luckily, they will also eagerly gobble up pieces of cut squid. Most experienced calico anglers with the luxury of access to live bait prefer to simply live-line their weightless offerings around the edges of the kelp so that it can swim freely and attract the attention of nearby predators.

When fishing for calicos in the kelp using artificial plastic baits, try starting out with colors that incorporate brown and golden hues with hologram or metal flake. Large Kalin grubs, and either single or double scampi-style tails sometimes work best. It is believed that these colors most closely emulate the appearance of juvenile kelp bass, which are regularly cannibalized by larger members of their own species. Classic, Fish Trap-style swimbaits also work well; but, because you must continually cast and retrieve them while trying different speeds and depths until you find the right combination, plastic artificials are not the best choice for lethargic anglers.

The fact remains that, if you work them properly, plastic swimbaits can mimic the movements of live baitfish with uncanny accuracy and sometimes end up catching more fish than live bait. Five-inch swimbaits are the best size to use when targeting calico bass in ocean waters. Once again, the most productive colors near the kelp are brown, olive, or gold with orange bellies. In open water and near rocky structure, I prefer using an anchovy or sardine pattern to try to provoke a strike.

Let the lure sink all the way down, then crank it back about a dozen times. Immediately throw your reel into free spool and let the lure sink back to the bottom. This system works well at anchor, but it's even better if you drift to cover more territory. When your line starts to slowly peel off, kick your reel into gear while winding as fast as possible to tighten the line and set the hook. If the fish swims into the kelp, put your reel back into free spool and wait about a minute before attempting to reel the fish in again. Often, it will have already swum back out from between the kelp strands on its own.

The colder the water temperature, the more likely it is that your lure will be attacked as it flutters down through the water column. While it is possible to catch calicos throughout the year, the best action takes place in spring and continues on through late summer.

During the warmest months, calico bass will often feed near surface bait schools, and bigger fish can be taken using a "surface iron" lure, which might normally be used to catch species such as yellowtail or big barracuda. Toss your jig directly over the kelp and begin retrieving it just before it hits the water to keep it from sinking. A slow, steady retrieve is the most effective way to keep your iron swimming properly. This may be a hard procedure to master, but there's nothing quite like the satisfaction of seeing a huge, trophy-size calico smash through the ocean's surface with your iron in its mouth.

Some anglers use hard baits such as Rebels, Rapalas, and Yo-Zuri plugs when going after calicos. This diligent type of cast-and-retrieve technique can be particularly deadly during the summer months if you observe fish crashing schools of bait. Resourceful anglers with small boats will often troll these same lures slowly past the perimeters of kelp, rocks, and other structure to enhance the size and quality of their catch. Despite the fact that this can be an extremely effective way to fish, it can also be quite hazardous, especially in thinly populated areas along the Baja coast. In the event of an emergency, anglers can quickly find themselves in need of help that will likely never arrive until it is too late.

Because calico bass are both territorial and delicious, their populations have diminished drastically during the past few decades, particularly in Southern California. Unless anglers in Baja practice great restraint, the same thing could happen south of the border. One simple practice could change all that. When you catch a kelp bass over 5 pounds, it is very important to release it unharmed. It's a well-known fact that large, female calicos are able to contribute millions more juveniles to rebuild their population than can smaller bass.

Fish weighing between 1 to 3 pounds are prolific, provide delightfully delicate fillets, and can be enjoyed without having such a negative impact on the resource. Of course, responsible anglers never keep more fish than they can use.

Sand Bass (*ParalabrAx nebulifer*)

The sand bass is one of the smaller members of the tropical grouper family that is found in the Pacific Ocean waters of northern Baja California. Although it can reach a weight of over 12 pounds, it is unusual to take one more than 8 pounds, and far more likely that anglers will catch sand bass in the 2- to 5-pound range. The barred sand bass is a good fighter and is high on the list of desired species.

Barred sand bass range along the Pacific coast from Santa Cruz, California to Bahía Magdalena, in Baja California Sur, and they also have a "gold-spotted" cousin *(Paralabrax auroguttatus)* in the upper portion of the Sea of Cortez. They tend to move in from deeper water in the early months of spring to spawn on the large expanses of mud flats or sand that lie just off the northern Baja coast. During these periods, they

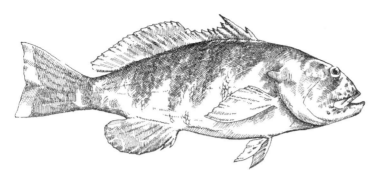

Sand bass (SCOTT KENNEDY)

begin to feed ravenously, and are not too particular about what they consume. Their spawning season extends through the fall months, after which time they migrate into deeper water. Sand bass can be caught throughout the year, but are most prolific during the summer months.

They can be found in water as shallow as 5 to 10 feet, but are far more commonly located in areas that are 30 to 60 feet deep. Sand bass can be taken on live or cut bait, but are often more susceptible to a properly presented artificial lure that resembles the natural baitfish and crustaceans upon which they normally feed.

One popular, effective, and durable lure for sand bass is the chrome spoon, particularly the Hopkins and the Krocodile by Luhr Jensen. Cast out the spoon and allow it to flutter down through the water column with a flashing action that looks like a wounded baitfish.

Sand bass will also attack passing swimbaits and grubs while holding in their usual poised, upward-facing position near the bottom. Plastic grubs in green, chartreuse, orange, pearl white, and occasionally hot pink work well. Swimbaits that incorporate blues and greens into their patterns are most likely to incite a strike. Swimbaits perform best if they're allowed to sink to the bottom and retrieved with the current. Grubs, however, are more effective if bounced along the bottom and over eelgrass beds.

Spotted Bay Bass
(Paralabrax maculatofasciatus)

The spotted bay bass is most commonly caught in bays and esteros in northerly areas of the Baja coast. They are gray to olive brown in color with round black spots over the entire body, head, and fins. The

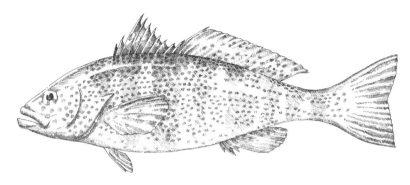

Spotted bay bass (SCOTT KENNEDY)

spotted bay and barred sand bass can be distinguished from the calico bass by the height of their third dorsal spine. In the spotted and barred basses, it is the longest of the dorsal spines, while in the calico bass that particular spine is of practically equal length as its others.

Spotted bay bass primarily target small forage fish and crustaceans

Hungry "spotties" will attack almost anything—in this case it was a freshwater spinnerbait. (BRANDON COTTON)

such as rock crabs and ghost shrimp, but also consume other organisms in their environment as well. They are most plentiful during the summer months, but can generally be taken in Baja waters throughout the year.

Clams and cut baits work well for catching spotted bay bass, but Carolina-rigged plastic grubs in weedy areas, and small spoons and swimbaits in open water can often be far more productive.

Leopard Grouper (Golden Grouper) (*Mycteroperca rosacea*)

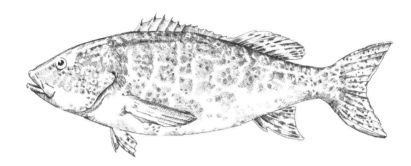

Leopard grouper (SCOTT KENNEDY)

Although some anglers mistake the common leopard grouper and its golden-phase counterpart for different species, they are actually the same fish. But only about 1 percent of leopard grouper ever display this color phase, which makes their entire bodies virtually radiate with a bright golden hue.

Leopard grouper are a staple of both commercial fishermen and recreational anglers, who target them on both sides of the peninsula between the midriff and the southern tip of Baja Sur. The firm, white, delicate fillets of the leopard grouper are extremely versatile in a number of different recipes and are considered gourmet table fare by almost everyone who has eaten them.

This fish can usually be found in waters around rocky terrain both inshore and adjacent to offshore islands at depths from 10 to nearly 200 feet. Like most other members of the grouper family, they are ambush feeders that make a habit of hanging out in their rock-strewn environment until an unsuspecting forage fish like a sardina or small mackerel swims by.

Because of this, it is imperative that anglers put a lot of pressure on leopard grouper once they have been securely hooked, and pull as hard as they can without breaking their line to pull the fish away from its hiding place before it has a chance to reposition itself inside the structure.

While using live bait is one of the easiest ways to attract interest from leopard grouper and numerous other species along the Baja coast, they will also viciously attack a variety of lures, including plastic lead-head jigs, chrome spoons, jointed iron, and slowly trolled hard baits like those manufactured by Rapala, Rebel, and Yo-Zuri.

Leopard grouper are territorial and can reach weights up to 50 pounds. They receive a lot of fishing pressure from both recreational and commercial contingents; hence, it is important to release all leopard grouper of less than 6 pounds in order to give those members of this slow-growing species an opportunity to grow to maturity and eventually reproduce.

Pacific Dog Snapper
(*Lutjanus Novemfasciatus*)

Pacific Dog Snapper (SCOTT KENNEDY)

Pacific dog snapper, also referred to as *pargo perro* in Baja, are generally caught from Bahía Tortugas on the Pacific side to Bahía de Los Angeles in the sea of Cortez.

In southern Baja, the moniker "pargo" can be used interchangeably to refer to different fish species, much as Californians might allude to certain members of the *Sebastes* family as being "red snapper" or "salmon grouper." On the southern half of the peninsula, Pacific dog snapper are members of the true snapper family, Lutjanidae. These fish are found close to islands, reefs, and rocky areas, and can range in

Known as *pargo perro* in Baja, big Pacific dog snapper can give you more fight than you can handle. (TAILHUNTER INTERNATIONAL)

size from 5 to well over 90 pounds. Most are prime table fare, but all seem to have the infuriating habit of grabbing a lure or bait and running straight into any nearby structure that happens to be handy.

When heading south for Pacific dog snapper, it is a good idea to bring along *at least* one 5-pound block of frozen squid. Carnada, or cut bait, also works—but there's a good reason why squid is often called "candy bait." Pacific dog snapper deserve your respect, and should be pursued with conventional tackle, and a line test of 25 pounds at a minimum. Making the unwise decision to use so-called "heavy-duty" spinning gear could easily ruin your day when targeting these stubborn and pugnacious fish.

A standard dropper loop is an effective setup, but I prefer using a whole squid on a modified trap-rig. If you've never made one before, first tie a large treble hook to the end of a 25- to 35-pound-test fluorocarbon leader about 25 to 30 inches long. Next tie on a single, No. 2/0 or other live bait hook corresponding with the size of the squid being used. Then tie the tag end of the leader to the middle eye a three-way swivel. Tie an 8-inch leader on the bottom eye, and attach a 4- to 6-ounce torpedo sinker to the terminal end. Hook one prong of the treble hook between the squid's eyes, and then pin the single live bait hook through its nose. As the squid is slowly lowered through the water column, it tends to flow off in the current, and almost looks as if it's swimming. Once you reach the bottom, give it about two cranks up and hang on to your rod!

I'll always remember my trip to a prominent East Cape resort a few years ago when the pangero first asked me what I wanted to fish for. His smile dropped noticeably when I enthusiastically chirped, *"Yo quiero pescando pargo perro!"* instead of the usual request for marlin and sailfish. He then raised his eyebrows in confusion when he saw my block of squid and the large treble hooks.

On the way to the fishing grounds just north of the Cabo Pulmo Reserve, he couldn't help but speak up. "Por favor, señor!" he finally interjected, "Your hooks are *much* too big!" He pleaded for me to change my rig, but I remained adamant.

On our first stop, less than 30 seconds from the moment I cranked my squid up from the bottom I got slammed, and suddenly found myself in a spirited battle with a 13-pound amberjack. Not exactly what I was shooting for, but a nice fish and a good fight all the same. Other boats that swarmed in on us after my catch sat soaking untouched sardinas, as I pulled in a 6-pound red snapper, and a chunky, barred Pacific dog snapper on my squid. Needless to say, my pangero made no further observations regarding my tackle or technique for the remainder of the trip.

Giant Black Sea Bass (*Stereolepis gigas*)

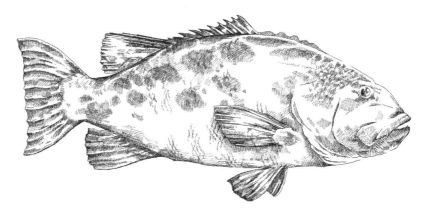

Black sea bass (SCOTT KENNEDY)

Nearly a century ago, perhaps the most exotic recreational pursuit that was offered to guests staying at the world famous Hotel del Coronado near San Diego was fishing for giant black sea bass off Mexico's nearby Coronado Islands. In fact, the hotel even made a habit of taking promotional and souvenir shots of visitors standing next to several of the then-common leviathans, holding a fishing rod that they may not have ever actually used.

The sport and commercial harvesting of these giant sea bass was prevalent within the state of California between 1870 and 1981. In 1982, the California State Legislature, together with the Fish and Game Commission, instituted a zero-take moratorium, while still allowing anglers who were returning from fishing in Mexico to be in possession of up to two fish per trip.

The once-thriving fishery for huge fish originally targeted fish in Southern California waters, but eventually moved south into northern Baja as the California populations began to decline. One of the most productive regions on the Pacific side of the peninsula remains the area between Punta Colonet and Magdalena, as well as in the Sea of Cortez between Loreto and Bahía Gonzaga. In the early days, commercial panga fishermen had to rely upon handlines, then later resorted to the use of gillnets as the species became harder to find on a predictable basis.

Unfortunately, abusive harvesting over a period of many decades took a heavy toll on this slow-growing species. In 1934, sport fishing landings along the Southern California coast brought in a seasonal catch of an incredible 861,498 pounds, which declined to a mere 3,666 pounds in the early 1980s prior to the moratorium. Most of the fishing activity took place between the Channel Islands off Santa Barbara south to Islas Los Coronados, just below the Mexican border.

Divers have also played an active role in the depletion of United States stocks of giant black sea bass. Originally, they would free-dive while spearfishing, which still gave the fish a bit of an advantage. But many quickly switched to using scuba gear after World War II. They were especially adept at exploiting spawning aggregations, since skilled divers had no trouble approaching them during their reproductive activities.

Even worse, once they had found a spawning aggregation, some divers would return on a daily basis until most of the fish had been taken. Limited information exists about the details of giant sea bass reproduction and movement, since this species has never been the subject of very many directed studies.

These days, the closest that most Southern California anglers have gotten to catching a member of the tropical grouper family is when they have hooked one of their distant cousins, such as a calico or sand bass. Up until the mid-1960s, however, there were healthy stocks of broomtail grouper and giant black sea bass thriving in rocky lairs along California's coastal islands between Santa Barbara and the Mexican border.

A few other members of the grouper family that are found off of the Baja coast are the spotted cabrilla, the gulf grouper, and the broom-tail grouper. The highly coveted black sea bass, however, are among the largest of the family. They grow to more than 7 feet in length, and fish well over 500 pounds have been recorded. Marine scientists project some of these monsters to be almost 100 years old.

Luckily, juvenile black sea bass are now once again occasionally being caught incidentally from southern California sport fishing boats and, although they still should be released immediately, this is a sign that bodes well for the future. Another positive indication of the healthy population increase of giant black sea bass in our area is the growing number of sightings from observers who have seen them swimming just off mainland beaches.

Baja California still supports a viable number of these fish, partic-ularly around the volcanic islands located in the mid to upper portion of the Sea of Cortez. This type of angling is the specialty of the moth-ership panga fishing businesses operating out of San Felipe.

On the Pacific side of the peninsula, the waters off of Bahía San Quintin are one well-known haunt for giant black sea bass. This fact adds to the ultimate challenge of catching and actually landing one.

One of the most effective techniques for catching larger grouper in-volves teamwork and cooperation. The skipper positions the boat within 50 yards of a likely grouper hole, and places the engine in neu-tral. The angler then drops over a bottom rig connected to an 80- to 100-pound-test fluorocarbon leader, which is baited with a live mack-erel. The line is kept tight with the weight on the bottom until the an-gler detects a pickup.

At this precise moment, the alert angler calls for the skipper to "hit it," at which time the captain throws the boat into gear and immedi-ately pulls away from the spot until the fish is too far from its rocky cavern to return. Once a big black sea bass is allowed to lodge itself back into its home, it is almost impossible to extricate.

When it comes to elegant table fare, there is nothing quite as de-lightful as a large, thick fillet of fresh black sea bass. The best eating fish are usually 150 pounds or less. The meat is firm, white, and tender with a delicate flavor that can sometimes be compared with fine shellfish. Bake it, sauté it in garlic butter, or grill it over mesquite. Unless you over-cook it, this is one type of fish that is difficult to prepare improperly.

For this very reason, when fishing in Baja, it is extremely impor-tant to release smaller fish as soon as they are caught so that they may have an opportunity to grow into much bigger ones. Black sea bass weighing 80 pounds or less are still considered juveniles, and should be quickly returned to the water.

Catching and landing one of these huge grouper can be the angling experience of a lifetime. But when fishing for them legally in Mexican waters, let your conscience be your guide.

Halibut (California and Cortez) (*Paralichthys californicus* and *Paralichthys aestuarius*)

California halibut (SCOTT KENNEDY)

Referred to as *lenguado* in Baja, these oversized members of the flounder family can grow to more than 60 pounds and are eclipsed in size only by their giant cousins, the northern Pacific and Atlantic halibuts, which often reach weights of several hundred pounds.

In addition to the California halibut on Baja California's Pacific coast, the Cortez halibut is found in the central to upper waters of the Sea of Cortez and has a more compact, less lengthy body than its more westerly counterpart.

Because there is no minimum size limit for taking these coveted fish in the waters of Baja California, it is always important to exercise restraint and remember that halibut generally must be over 20 inches in length before they can first spawn.

These flat, opportunistically aggressive predators are masters of camouflage. Their coloration will often change from dark brown to golden sandstone, depending on their cover, and they can deftly wiggle under the loose sand and lie motionless with little more exposed than the two eyes on the topside of their bodies. Suddenly, when a smaller, unsuspecting fish swims by, the halibut explodes forth with open jaws and a flurry of pointed, slashing teeth to devour its prey.

During spring through late fall, this was one of my favorite target species. Fishing for the California halibut along Baja Norte's Pacific coast can be exceptional, especially in the various sandy, inshore areas that make excellent spawning grounds for this species. Since these months tend to spark interludes of the halibut's reproductive activities, those windows of time are usually most productive for the anglers who seek them out. On the Pacific side, bays such as Bahía de Todos Santos and Bahía San Quintin are also good places to find halibut. Schools of forage fish such as smelt and anchovies are found in these areas and help to attract larger halibut that move in seasonally to spawn.

While fishing for lenguado using natural baits, it is not unusual to experience many short or missed bites. This situation can be addressed by using a "trap rig." To construct a trap rig, tie a small treble hook to the end of a 12- to 20-pound-test fluorocarbon leader approximately 25 inches long, and attach a single live bait hook about 4 to 5 inches up from the treble. Then tie the leader to the middle eye of a three-way swivel, and attach a 2-, 4-, or 6-ounce torpedo sinker on a 5-inch leader to the bottom eye with a clip swivel. Tie the line coming from your rod and reel to the third eye of the swivel, and the trap rig is now complete and ready to use. Place one prong of the treble hook in the tail of the baitfish, and the live bait hook through its nose.

Live bait is one of the most efficient methods for catching halibut, either from a boat or onshore. Top smelt are one of the halibut's favorite meals, and can be caught around rock jetties, pilings, and marina docks by chumming with very small bits of bread, and then using a Lucky Joe or Sabiki bait rig to hook them. Smelt are much hardier than anchovies, and can stay alive for a longer period of time when kept in a bait bucket or tank. The same bait rigs are also effective in taking small mackerel, which are a prime offering for bigger flatties. Sometimes catching your own bait may not be practical, and if that's the case, another option is to buy salted anchovies from a bait and tackle store and keep them on ice.

Halibut can also be taken on white or squid-colored "jointed iron" lures, as well as on 3- to 5-inch plastic swimbaits in colors like blue or green that resemble local forage fish such as smelt, sardines, or anchovies. They will also attack plastic grubs of a similar length, with the best colors generally being chartreuse, orange, or green. Grubs in smoke or clear colors with high metal flake content are also effective.

When fishing from a beach or rocky outcropping, gently cast your rig out as far as possible onto the sandy bottom, then let it move along with the tidal flow. When fishing from a boat, always lower live or dead bait rigs to the bottom slowly to prevent them from becoming tangled by a too-quick descent.

When a bite occurs, gently lift the tip of your rod until weight or movement is detected, then set the hook with a light touch. Keep pressure on the fish throughout the retrieve, but make sure that your drag is not set too tight. Remember that halibut have relatively soft mouths, which can easily cause the fish to be lost if anglers become overly aggressive.

The California halibut is one of the most avidly pursued gamefish on Baja's northern Pacific coast and is highly prized as a gourmet delicacy. When properly cleaned, it can yield up to 70 percent of its body weight in mild, delicate fillets.

To get the highest yield from these fish, use a very sharp knife and begin the filleting process by cutting a lengthwise line down the middle of the halibut's back. Then carefully separate each of the two sections of meat from the skeletal structure directly below them with evenly measured incisions that scrape cleanly across the bones. After removing the skin from each fillet, turn the fish over and perform the same procedure on its white underbelly.

One of my all-time favorite ways to prepare halibut fillets is to coat each piece lightly in flour, shaking off any excess. Dip them in beaten egg yolk, and then dredge in crushed macadamia nuts. Make sure that each piece is covered completely. Place the fillets in a buttered baking casserole, and then drizzle each fillet with a tablespoon of melted butter. Bake on the center rack of a preheated, 450-degree oven for 10 to 15 minutes. Serve with fresh lemon wedges.

California Sheephead
(*Semicossyphus pulcher*)

The California sheephead is a hermaphrodite. It begins life as a female, and then becomes male later in its development. This fish also happens to be the largest member of the wrasse family in our hemisphere, with record specimens that weigh in at well over 30 pounds. Sheephead are

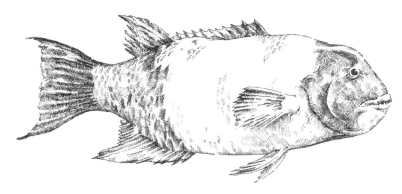

California sheephead (SCOTT KENNEDY)

generally found in rocky, kelp-filled inshore waters between 20 and 100 feet in depth, although they have been caught at depths of nearly 200 feet.

For years, the California sheephead was considered to be a marginally desirable species and, at times, even a bit of a pest by sport anglers in pursuit of more glamorous quarry. That was before people started to realize how easily its alabaster white fillets could be turned

The California sheephead is a colorful and tasty member of the inshore marine community off the Baja coast. (STEVE LONHART)

into gourmet table fare. I vividly remember the first occasion this fact was brought to my attention.

It was a sunny, summer day in the early 1960s while my dad and I were happily slamming calico bass aboard a sport fishing boat working the kelp just off the coast of Ensenada. After inadvertently hooking a colorful California sheephead, I loudly exclaimed, "Damn *goat!*" mimicking the response that I had observed so many times while watching older anglers and deckhands during many fishing trips on southern California cattle boats.

Moments after it hit the deck, I drew back my foot as if to kick the fish, but was quickly stopped by a nearby deckhand. "Oh, *no*, my friend!" He offered encouragingly, placing his hand on my shoulder. "This fish is no "chivo" . . . and if you throw it away, you will be making a *beeg* mistake!" He winked at us in a friendly, knowing manner. "Do you like crab?" He queried.

"Who doesn't?" I quipped with a touch of adolescent sarcasm.

"Well, this is how you can turn your "goat" into crabmeat . . . or, at least something that tastes a *lot* like it!" He then proceeded to explain how to cut off the thick fillets with the skin side on, and then steam, chill, and flake the delicate meat into a large bowl. Our knowing deckhand then suggested adding some finely chopped green onions, cilantro, celery, chunky salsa, and several shrimp to create a batch of seafood cocktails that we would never forget.

Our sheephead went immediately into the sack, and we followed his instructions to the letter after we got back home. Luckily, there were some cocktail shrimp in the freezer, and we had nearly everything else on hand that he had mentioned. The resulting cocktail was a toothsome masterpiece, and the deckhand's recipe has now been in our family cookbook for decades.

Although this species is found from Cabo San Lucas north to California's Monterey Bay, it is uncommon north of Point Conception. There is also an isolated population of these bucktoothed fish inside the Gulf of California. Their diet consists primarily of crabs, mussels, squid, sea cucumbers, and sea urchins. They use their large, caninelike teeth to pry food from reefs and rocks, while a special plate in their throat crushes the shells into small pieces for easy digestion.

Sheephead will take a variety of live and cut baits, such as anchovy or squid that is fished on or near the bottom. Giant sheephead have been known to eat live mackerel, but few realize that a couple of other hot sheephead baits are live freshwater crayfish and common garden snails.

Bonito (*Sarda chiliensis*)

Pacific bonito (SCOTT KENNEDY)

Pacific bonito are among the smallest members of the tuna family, and can usually be found along the Southern California and Baja coasts from late spring through early winter. In the Sea of Cortez, another bonito species (*Sarda orientalis*) is present, which is quite similar to its cousin in the Pacific. While bonito are spirited fighters, they were not particularly well thought of as a food fish for many decades. I'll never forget when I was a teenager back in the 1960s and used to call them every degrading name I could think of, and would then disrespectfully refer to them as "cat food" every time one would come over the boat's rail.

With the rapidly increasing popularity of sushi and sashimi, however, the bonito has finally gained new respect. When properly handled and extremely fresh, wafer-thin slices of its translucent, white flesh are considered a gourmet delicacy when served along with a little wasabi and shoyu. And knowledgeable Baja anglers have always known how delicious fresh bonito can be when it has been smoked.

If possible, one of the very best techniques for making sure that your bonito will turn out great as table fare—no matter how you prepare it—is to bleed the fish out, gut it, and throw it under ice as soon as it is off your hook. Looking back, it is no wonder why some anglers got a bad impression about the eating quality of bonito after their catch had been thrown into a burlap sack and left to sit out on a boat deck in the hot sun until it returned to port.

Bonito are excellent fighters and, once a school is aroused, they will viciously attack a variety of lures and baits. Most Pacific bonito are taken by a using a combination of trolling and live bait fishing methods. Schools of bonito are often found by trolling and, once located, live baitfish or lures can be used while drifting nearby to catch even more fish. Bonito are generally found offshore in 300 to 600 feet of water, but can also be encountered in the vicinity of kelp beds. The maximum weight of a Pacific bonito is just over 20 pounds, but most anglers end up catching school-size fish between 4 and 8 pounds.

Pacific bonito have 10 or 11 stripes on their backs running from the dorsal fin, and 15 or more below their gills. They are usually found anywhere from coastal inshore waters to more than 100 miles offshore, and range from Vancouver Island, British Columbia to Baja California Sur. These fish generally travel in schools and are likely to be caught by trolling or drift fishing with live baits near active congregations.

Chumming for bonito can be very effective, particularly along the outer edges of kelp beds during the summer months. Once a few bonito have been attracted, many more may quickly converge on the area to investigate the flurry of activity.

The best live baits for bonito are anchovies or sardines, but they will also attack Krocodile-style chrome spoons, small Rapalas, and medium-weight surface iron in blue-and-white or chrome.

California Barracuda (*Sphyraena argentea*)

Pacific barracuda (SCOTT KENNEDY)

Pacific barracuda are an open-ocean species usually found along the Pacific coast during the summer. Although they prefer live bait, they can also be taken on chrome spoons, topwater poppers, and surface iron in a blue and chrome combination. The barracuda has a slim body design, and rarely exceeds 10 pounds. They offer a respectable fight on light to medium tackle, and grow to a maximum length of about 4 feet. The Pacific barracuda can be distinguished from barracuda found in the Sea of Cortez by its silvery sides and a lack of bars or spots.

When schools of hungry barracuda are present, it can be extremely difficult to get live bait and lures past the barracuda so that they can be attacked by other species. Since the Pacific barracuda is not held in particularly high esteem as a food fish, most anglers eschew it—unless hooking up with one means that they don't get "skunked" because they've caught nothing else on that particular fishing trip.

Pacific Sierra Mackerel
(*Scomberomorus sierra*)

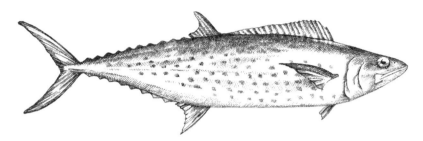

Sierra mackerel (SCOTT KENNEDY)

Its slim, streamlined body and viciously sharp teeth make the Pacific sierra one of the most effective predatory species that swims in the waters of Baja California, rivaled only by the wahoo, which is also a member of the mackerel family. Both these fishes make a living out of slashing their way through unsuspecting schools of baitfish, and then casually coming back to consume the leftover chunks of uneaten prey that are sinking slowly toward the bottom.

Anglers visiting from other regions, particularly the Southeast and the Gulf Coast of the United States, will occasionally confuse Baja's sierra with Spanish mackerel. Once hooked, sierra make long runs and fight hard but are often lost when their razor-sharp teeth come in contact with an angler's line. For this reason, it can be a good idea to use a wire leader, although doing so can drastically diminish the number of strikes you receive.

Some of the very best fishing for sierra usually occurs in predawn and early morning hours in less that 75 feet of water over a structured bottom. This is one species that can be a heck of a lot of fun on medium-light tackle or fly gear. Live bait is great if you happen to have it, but the sierra is so voracious that it really isn't necessary, especially when they are hungry. My favorite lure for this kind of fishing is probably the Krocodile spoon, since it can be easily cast into the middle of a feeding frenzy and then allowed to flutter slowly down through the water column like a wounded or dying baitfish. Under these conditions, a wild and gluttonous sierra will nearly always eagerly inhale your lure.

Once caught, immediately dressed out, and placed on ice, the sierra can be delicious, especially when made into ceviche. But the most important thing to remember if you want to enjoy it at peak flavor and texture is to take care of your fish as soon as it's landed, and then eat it the same day that you caught it; sierra does not keep or freeze well.

Wahoo (*Acanthocybium solandri*)

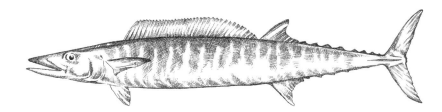

Wahoo (SCOTT KENNEDY)

Sometimes called "the tiger of the sea," the wahoo is a lightning-fast, sharp-toothed predator that epitomizes the eat-or-be-eaten law of the jungle that exists in the waters surrounding the Baja peninsula. It is also one of the world's most revered food fish.

Early Hawaiian islanders gave it the name *ono*, which translates roughly as "good to eat"; and the wahoo certainly fits that description. Its comparison to a tiger is prompted not only by its powerful jaws and vicious nature, but also by the two dozen or so semivertical dark blue striped markings on its sides.

This glamorous cousin to the Atlantic king mackerel can be caught intermittently off both coasts of Baja Sur during the warmest months of the year, when coastal waters can reach nearly bathlike temperatures. Their annual appearance can be unpredictable, with a fantastic wahoo catch one year and practically none migrating into range the next. And things can get particularly frustrating when it comes to trying to hook and land one.

Trolling for wahoo is usually done at speeds of 10 to 12 knots, rather than the 7 to 8 knots used to troll for many other gamefish species. Veteran wahoo anglers all have their favorite lures—sometimes it's a Marauder, sometimes its a homemade "wahoo bomb," but no matter what kind of artificial bait you select, the most effective, all-around combination of colors seems to be purple and black. But don't forget to incorporate a strong wire leader, or your chances of actually bringing one over the rail are rather slim.

Your easiest job in the process of harvesting a wahoo from the waters of Baja will be in selecting a method to cook and enjoy it; it is delicious barbecued, baked, sautéed, steamed, or enjoyed as sushi or sashimi. As long as is isn't overcooked, it is delectable prepared in almost any way that you can think of.

Roosterfish (Pez Gallo) (*Nemtistius pectoralis*)

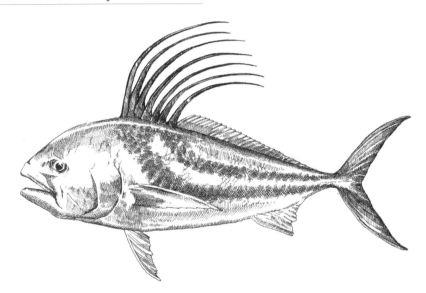

Roosterfish (SCOTT KENNEDY)

Roosterfish, or pez gallo as they are called south of the border, are one of the premier glamour species of the Baja coast. Their most striking feature is the large, almost ungainly, roosterlike dorsal fin that both inspired its name and allows anglers to easily detect when it is foraging for baitfish close to the surface. Roosterfish are caught exclusively along the Pacific shorelines of Mexico and Central America, with the majority of the catch taking place in the Sea of Cortez. The best time of year to target roosterfish is between May and October.

Roosters are a prime target of many fly anglers along the East Cape of Baja Sur, but these fish can also fall victim to a properly placed live

The roosterfish, or pez gallo, is one of the most coveted gamefish in all of Baja Sur. (TAILHUNTER INTERNATIONAL)

bait. Once hooked, roosterfish put on a premier battle that is characterized by long, drag-burning runs, which eventually dissipate in intensity as the fish runs out of steam.

Although a noble gamefish, the pez gallo is not a prime contender as table fare. Its flesh is dark, unappealing, and strongly flavored. As a result, the roosterfish is a perfect candidate for a remorseless catch-and-release.

Barred Surfperch
(*Amphistichus argenteus*)

During the first few months of each calendar year, when the cold rain from northern storms batters Baja's upper Pacific coast, the surf remains churned up into a heavy froth and water temperatures tend to plummet into the low to mid-50s. It is a season when many anglers have already turned their attention toward getting their tackle ready for the happily anticipated action in spring, which is only a few months

Barred surfperch (SCOTT KENNEDY)

away. This is also a time when record high lunar tides occur, causing incoming waves to encroach much farther up the beach than normal.

For those hardy souls willing to roll up their pants legs and wade into the crisp shore break with light tackle in hand, these periods also create prime conditions for catching barred surfperch, or mojarra as they are referred to south of the border. Actually, the same name is applied to just about every perchlike fish in Baja. Southern Californians will often fish for them from piers and breakwaters, but in Baja California these amenities rarely exist, and surfperch are usually targeted by casting from shore.

In the off-season, Baja Norte's Pacific coast experiences very little pressure from shore anglers. Since some of the most productive surfperch spots are found several miles from the city and are a bit primitive, don't be surprised if you happen to get lucky and end up taking home a nice stringer of these popular, pan-size fish.

Sizable schools of barred surfperch can usually be found in the surf zone along most sandy beaches, where they tend to congregate in depressions or troughs along the soft bottom. In colder months, larger adults weighing up to 3 pounds come close to shore during their winter spawning cycle.

The most popular natural bait for mojarra is the soft-shelled sand crab, but local mussels and small pieces of cut anchovy can also be productive. When sand crabs are present, groupings of their small, filamentlike antenna can be seen protruding from the wet sand left behind by the tidal ebb. Digging beneath them immediately after a wave recedes will often produce several of these small, oval crustaceans. The ones that carry an orange egg sack under their carapaces tend to catch more fish.

Those who prefer fishing with bait should use either a standard, two-tiered surf-fishing setup or a Carolina rig, which is constructed by attaching a No. 4 or No. 6 treble hook to the end of a 4- to 6-pound-test fluorocarbon leader about 20 inches in length. Then tie a barrel swivel to the opposite end of the leader, and pass the line from your reel through a $\frac{1}{2}$- to 1-ounce egg sinker, and tie the line to the other eye of the swivel so that the sinker sits positioned above the leader. Beware, however, because barred surfperch are masterful bait thieves.

This same type of rig is also extremely deadly when using appropriately colored plastic grubs, which mimic the appearance of small crustaceans such as ghost shrimp and sand crabs. Watch the waves, and cast your lure just past the suds in the last swell of each incoming set immediately after it breaks.

One on my favorite techniques is to fish near a place where a sandy beach abruptly ends near rocky outcroppings or tide pools. Look for places where you can safely make your way out onto the structure and position yourself a few hundred yards away from the shoreline. You can then cast parallel to the breakers and work your lure or bait along the surf line for a better shot at foraging fish. These areas can also provide an occasional opportunity to hook up with larger inshore species such as halibut, bass, corbina, or even white sea bass.

Some of the best locations to fish for mojarra in Baja are the sandy beaches between Rosarito, La Mission, and the beach south of the La Salina Marina jetties. The shorelines adjoining the outer mouth of Ensenada's Punta Banda Estero and the small patch of sandy beach south of La Bufadora at Puerto Escondido are also good, as are similar areas farther south that punctuate the coast to points well past Bahía San Quintin.

Although barred surfperch weigh only between 4 ounces and 3 pounds, they are still prized by many of the anglers who pursue them, and are perhaps the most likely species to end up over a beach campfire in Baja. They can be filleted, or simply gutted, scaled, and cooked whole. Whichever way you chose to dress them out, they are usually best either pan-fried or steamed. Once their cooked, snowy-white meat is flaked away from the bones, you are left with mild, delicate, and tender morsels that will receive a unanimous thumbs-up from the hungry guests around your dinner table.

California Corbina (*Menticirrhus undulatus*)

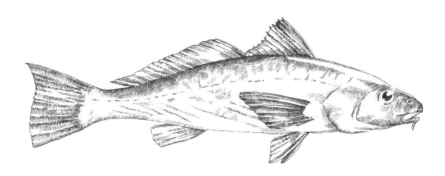

California corbina (SCOTT KENNEDY)

As summertime water temperatures along Baja Norte's Pacific coast reach the high 60s and low 70s, corbina will begin to go on a feeding rampage in the surf near sandy beaches. Their high, silver and bronze humped backs can often be seen protruding from the shallow shore break in a mere 6 inches of water as they grub for sand crabs in the few, fleeting moments before the wave recedes. These hard-fighting, gourmet-quality fish are members of the croaker family, and are among the most elusive species along the Pacific coast of Baja.

Many beaches in Baja Norte offer excellent corbina fishing during the late summer and fall, but relatively few anglers take advantage of it. Uncountable niches, coves, and hidden areas with sand and surf feature great corbina action just waiting to be enjoyed.

All that's required to get in on the fun is a light-action spinning rod, a reel spooled with 4- to 6-pound-test line, a few split-shot, and a No. 6 to No. 10 live bait or treble hook. Freshly caught sand crabs are one of the most effective natural baits, and are often available right at your feet. As you walk down the beach, watch the areas where the surf has just ebbed. You may notice wet patches of sand that look a bit rough compared to the smoother areas around them. This is usually an indication that sand crabs are immediately below the surface. If you dig in these spots as soon as they are exposed, you will often be able to catch all the bait you need.

While feeding corbina will readily consume sand crabs, anglers who cast small, shrimp-pattern flies and tiny plastic grubs into the surf can also expect one of these fish to hungrily snatch it up. They are easily spooked, and often swim much closer to shore than you would ever suspect. Sight fishing is a good way to locate corbina, so always keep an eye out for foraging corbina, which move slowly and stop occasionally. Look for this activity in shallow, onshore surf no more than 2 to 3 feet deep.

When the corbina action is hot, blind casting can also be effective. Wade into the surge until the water meets your leg just below the knee, and then target your casts at an angle that is practically parallel to the surf line and into the sandy depressions that have been created by the wave action. You will often have the best chance of provoking a strike by lightly twitching your lure or bait while retrieving it at a sometimes painfully slow pace.

Once a corbina takes your offering, try to set the hook in the same manner as would a fly angler. Hold the line in one hand and your rod in the other, and then cast as you release the line in a sweeping motion. Remember that fishing for corbina is a finesse game, and losing your patience can also mean losing your fish.

No matter what type of reel you use, don't forget to set the drag very lightly. The best line weight to take corbina ranges between 2- and 6-pound-test at the very most, which can snap in a heartbeat if you make the unwise decision to get into a tug-of-war with a fat corbina. But keep your line tight and slack free for an additional advantage while setting the hook.

When fighting a hooked fish, wade out into shallow water and keep the rod tip up, while letting the fish run against the slight resistance provided by the drag. Be sure to back up and reel the fish all the way up onto the beach before attempting to touch it or the line near its mouth. Otherwise, it might be only barely hooked and, with a few flips of its tail, may find an opportunity to come unbuttoned and swim away before you can actually land it.

Fishing the surf during early morning or late afternoon on an incoming tide is often your best bet, with outgoing tides producing good action to a somewhat lesser degree. Keep in mind that, when targeting corbina, your bait or lure must be worked where the fish are feeding—don't expect them to come looking for it. If it drifts away from a potentially productive area, reel in and repeat the process.

When a corbina is sighted, be sure to maintain a low profile by casting and retrieving from a slightly stooped position so that you can stay out of the wily corbina's field of vision. Keep your rod tip low, and pointed toward the fish to minimize visibility, as well as to provide better positioning for a possible hook set.

Baja's Changing Marine Life:
The Old Versus The New

The Totuava or Totoaba (*Cynoscion macdonaldi*):
The Sad Loss of a Noble Species and a Valuable Resource

In the early years of the 20th century, San Felipe was little more than a remote, tiny poblado at the northern end of the Sea of Cortez. Few people north of the border even knew that it existed, let alone entertained the thought of ever going there. The rare exceptions were dedicated anglers in pursuit of the mightiest croaker of them all, the giant totuava, which had also become the backbone of San Felipe's economy.

These fish easily attained weights of several hundred pounds. Totuava were considered gourmet table fare and were a staple of fish markets in Southern California from the late 1920s to the beginning of World War II. Unfortunately, the many dams built along the Colorado River in the 1930s reduced its southernmost extremity, the Rio Hardy, to a virtual trickle. This so depleted the flow of fresh water into the region that it negatively impacted the previously perfect balance of brackishness that had supported a healthy seasonal spawn of the totuava for eons.

There was also a skyrocketing demand for desiccated totuava livers in the Asian marketplace, back in the days before any type of dependable refrigerated transportation was available. Tragically, during these years the beaches around San Felipe were often strewn with hundreds of eviscerated carcasses of these huge fish, which were uncaringly left to rot under the blazing desert sun. This unforgivable waste, along with the excessive bottom trawling for shrimp that disturbed development of totuava in the larval stage, began to spell doom for the noble totuava.

By the late 1950s, local commercial fishing interests found that the waning totuava resources made it almost impossible for them to meet the needs of the market by employing conventional fishing techniques. This realization, teamed with a pathetic ignorance of marine ecology, prompted the commercial fishermen to start using explosives to stun and kill the big totuava that they were now having a difficult time taking by hook and line.

Fortunately, by the early 1960s, the Mexican government began to intervene, although many will opine that their actions were both too little and too late. But by the end of the decade, the once thriving sport fishing industry that had been built on the recreational pursuit of totuava had collapsed and, in the mid-1970s, Mexico's Oficina de Pesca placed a total moratorium on both commercial and recreational take of totuava. The good news is that, with current aggressive husbandry and habitat enhancement efforts, the totuava is starting to make a comeback. Sadly, however, stocks will probably never return to the number and size common during San Felipe's glory days, when totuava were able to reach weights of over 300 pounds.

Today, there is mounting pressure to sell special permits that would allow recreational anglers to purchase a one-take tag to legally fish for the species, but there is a fair amount of resistance to this idea, particularly among marine biologists who are familiar with the totuava's somewhat disturbing history. Many of them believe that its lurid tale of demise is a perfect, textbook example of how human impact nearly caused the complete extinction of a prime fish species.

Don't get me wrong, the region around San Felipe still offers many great opportunities to catch a variety of fish, including orangemouth corbina, shortfin corvina, and spotted bay bass. Fishing from shore can also be productive during periods of good tidal movement, and if you don't have your own boat, a commercial panga can be booked right on the beach. There are even a few charters that take passengers just offshore to Consag Rock, where many larger species are often available.

Farther south along the coast toward Puertecitos, the long stretches of sandy beach are a kayak angler's dream, and catches of big orangemouth corbina are not uncommon during summer. But one thing is certain: no matter how many times I go there, I never visit San Felipe without taking along my fishing rod.

The Giant Humboldt Squid (*Dosidicus gigas*): The Mysterious Appearance of a Giant

While the smaller, market-size squid, *Loligo opalescens*, is probably the most commonly recognized species of cephalopod, the giant Humboldt squid is an entirely different character altogether; it is a tenacious brute with an extremely wicked reputation. The species can reach a length of over 6 feet, and is known for its aggressive, predatory nature. The Humboldt squid has incredibly powerful tentacles and excellent underwater vision, as well as a razor-sharp beak that can easily tear through the flesh of its prey—or that of an unsuspecting angler.

Visions of malevolent giant squid were first created in the minds of readers well over 100 years ago by Jules Verne in his classic novel

The giant Humboldt squid is a relative newcomer to the waters surrounding Baja California. (TAILHUNTER INTERNATIONAL)

20,000 Leagues Under the Sea. Today, one thing is certain: there are far more giant Humboldt squid along both sides of Baja California and the California coastline than ever before in recorded history. Could this unusual situation be the ultimate realization of Verne's literary dream of a time when giant squid would take over the seas?

One manifestation of this phenomenon occurred in 2004, when a team of scientists led by Dr. William F. Gilly of Stanford University's Hopkins Marine Station, left on a 73-foot fishing boat to retrace the historic voyage made by renowned author John Steinbeck and his good friend Dr. Ed Ricketts, in 1940. The original boat, *The Western Flyer,* was a 76-foot purse seiner, which carried Ricketts, Steinbeck, his wife Carol, and their crew on a voyage that none of them would ever forget. The trip was chronicled in Steinbeck's subsequent book, *The Log of the Sea of Cortez.*

Jon Christensen, a science writer and Steinbeck Fellow at San José State University, also traveled on the 2004 expedition to document the journey on a daily basis. Although more than a half century separated the two voyages, aside from a progressive decrease in numbers, most of the various marine species that both exploratory groups observed were very much the same.

There was, however, one glaring difference. At absolutely no point in Steinbeck's detailed account of his trip did he ever mention the giant Humboldt squid. On the other hand, Christensen recently noted that these large cephalopods are now extremely common in the Sea of Cortez. As a matter of fact, sometimes they are so prolific that they have become pests to anglers targeting other species.

Since the Humboldt squid is also a prized food resource, there are some who don't view the recent burgeoning of the species as a negative event. Each year, hundreds of Mexican fishermen work fish in rough seas in small pangas for these big squid. It's no easy task, since the catch is very heavy and each squid must be caught on a handline. The entire economy of many Baja fishing poblados, like Santa Rosalia, depends upon the squid, with fishing and packing operations providing the majority of local jobs.

Today, recreational anglers have also discovered the sport and table value of this monstrous creature, albeit usually as an alternative catch to more conventional and popular species. Those who target Humboldt squid generally do so during the dark of night. Multiple, pre-mounted 300- to 500-watt lamps, preferably halogen, are used to draw the marauding beasts toward the boat. Once they have arrived, steady chumming with chunks of mackerel or squid will usually keep them hanging around.

Although they can sometimes be caught with bait or on various fishing lures, serious ocean hunters who specifically target these nasty boys know that they need special equipment to get the job done most effectively. In addition to a 3- to 6-foot length of multistrand, 150-pound-test (or stronger) wire leader to prevent the Humboldt's sharp beak from quickly separating the terminal tackle from the main line, a specially designed squid jig is also used. These lures have numerous pinlike prongs running up and down the body, which ensnare the tentacles of the giant squid as soon as they wrap around the artificial bait. The squid jigs come in different sizes; the large ones to descend down to deeper squid, and the smaller ones work well when they are near the surface.

Nothing likes being hooked, and the giant Humboldt squid is no exception . . . but it has a lot more weight to throw around than most of the fish that you might commonly catch. It also possesses a large sack of ink that should be allowed to discharge at boatside prior to gaffing the squid and hoisting it over the rail. Once the squid hits the deck, cut away and discard its head and tentacles and then place the body on ice to maintain its quality. Please, however, observe this important word of caution: *Avoid all contact with the large beak at the center of the tentacles!* Mangled or severed fingers are often the steep price paid by those who fail to observe this precaution.

On the other side of the coin, anglers who successfully fish for Humboldt squid are often happily rewarded with several pounds of gourmet calamari steak for the dinner table. For those who find themselves in this enviable situation but are not familiar with ways to prepare the delicacy, allow me to offer the following suggestions. First and foremost, do *not* overcook it! Overcooking squid—and most other seafood, for that matter—will result in it becoming tough, rubbery, and inedible.

To enjoy a wonderful calamari dinner, simply dip a thick fillet into beaten egg and then dredge it in Japanese panko-style breadcrumbs. Lightly sauté the steak in a mixture of butter, extra-virgin olive oil, and minced garlic, turning only once, until both sides are golden brown. Serve with lemon wedges, your favorite fresh vegetable, and rice or pasta on the side. It's that easy.

I'm no marine biologist, but when it comes to figuring out why the west coast of North America is seeing such a proliferation of giant Humboldt squid, it's apparent that you don't have to be a scientist to realize that the "experts" still don't fully understand good ol' Mother Earth.

For all our sakes, I certainly hope that sometime in the near future they do. In the meantime, I plan to take advantage of my blessings, pop open a bottle of crisp, chilled Chardonnay, and fry up a bunch of fresh, tasty calamari steaks!

Terminal Tackle and Fishing Suggestions 3

Onshore

In some remote coastal areas of Baja, there may be no viable, safe access to launch private craft, not even a small raft or kayak. In such places, anglers have an opportunity to understand what ancient tribal residents had to deal with on a daily basis for centuries while trying to wrest survival from the sea and the surrounding landscape. Those who want to fish these areas must rely upon stealth and their hunter-gatherer instincts a bit more than in most other fishing venues.

One of the first things to remember, especially around rocky outcroppings and tide pools, is that there are usually several types of fish living within a few yards of the water's edge. Most of these species rely heavily upon the marine organisms that live nearby, so the most effective baits that you can use to catch them could literally be available at your very feet.

Mussels, clams, limpets, crabs, ghost shrimp, and other crustaceans collected near where you plan to fish are all prime natural baits that, whether used on a sandy beach or near rocky structure, can provoke a strike faster that anything else you could offer. Of course, those with the foresight to bring along plenty of frozen squid or anchovies as well will stack the odds in their favor.

Generally speaking, one of the best rigs to use for this type of fishing is the standard dropper loop, which features an appropriately sized weight at the terminal end, and one or two hooks placed up the main line on single, double-tied loops about 18 inches from each other. When fishing from the rocks, never use more weight than is absolutely necessary. When possible, even try casting baits such as half-shelled mussels or clams and then let them sink slowly through the water column. The idea, of course, is to avoid getting hung up and losing your tackle.

Artificial baits can also work well when cast from shore and retrieved slowly with an occasional twitch, especially soft plastic grubs and swimbaits that mimic local forage fish, shrimp, and other similar organisms found in the area where you happen to be fishing.

At times when particularly aggressive and toothy species, such as halibut, sierra, or sea bass are present, shiny Krocodile-style spoons can be absolutely deadly reaction baits that can have your rod going "bendo" in a heartbeat when the fish are hungry.

Inshore

In Baja, you can fish inshore even from a surfboard. All this means is that you are no longer fishing from shore or a land-based platform, and are within about a mile or so of the coastline.

One of the most popular and effective ways of fishing inshore in Baja is from a sit-on-top kayak. Aluminum boats are also great, but all except the small cartoppers require either some kind of launch ramp or hard, stable shoreline to get them in and out of the water.

The best thing about fishing close to shore in a small boat or kayak is that you are able to work your baits and lures in "no-man's-land." These are areas that are too far out to be reached even by a long-distance surfcaster, but are also either too shallow or too close to shore for larger sportfishing boats to dare encroach therein.

When fishing inshore, catching your own live baits such as smelt or small mackerel with a Lucky Joe or Sabiki-style bait rig can sometimes give you an advantage on the water, especially when the baits are live-lined to fish that are actively feeding on the surface. Nonetheless, artificial baits can come into play as very potent tools for catching fish in these waters as well.

At depths between 10 and 90 feet, plastic grubs and swimbaits can be devastatingly effective on numerous species of gamefish when drifted slowly along the bottom. The only areas along the Baja coast where I have found them frustratingly ineffective are the places where triggerfish tend to proliferate. Triggerfish can slice up and destroy plastic swimbaits—without getting hooked themselves—faster than any other fish I have ever encountered. If you should find yourself in this type of situation, simply change to either a shiny chrome spoon or a one-piece or jointed metal jig to alleviate the problem.

Inshore trolling can also be extremely effective. Whether you're using hardbait or stickbait artificials such as Rapalas, Rebels, or Yo-Zuris, or pulling live or rigged baitfish, inshore trolling is more likely to be done at slower speeds, about 3 to 5 knots, as opposed to the speeds employed to catch bigger and faster gamefish offshore.

Offshore

Boats that are capable of venturing several miles off the Baja coast have access to even more exotic catches. The most popular gamefish, such as marlin, tuna, dorado, and wahoo are available offshore, and the boats that target them are also usually equipped with the latest electronic fish-finding equipment along with big bait tanks. These craft will usually also have the supplies and amenities onboard to stay out on the water for several days if necessary.

On the open sea, if they are not detected by the skipper's electronics, schools of fish are often found by seeking out working flocks of birds that are circling and diving on a particular spot, or by blind trolling at speeds between 7 and 10 knots until you get a hook-up.

Some of the best artificial baits for offshore trolling are brightly feathered jetheads and "hoochies" run either singly or in daisy chains. Once a fish is hooked on the troll, the crew will usually start chumming with chunks of bait to keep fish in the area and give other anglers aboard a chance to get their lines in the water also.

Unless you happen have your own boat—22 feet or more—and are also extremely familiar with the waters that you plan to fish, I would always strongly suggest that you hire a licensed captain to take you fishing offshore in Baja.

A Word about Fishing Kayaks and Inflatables

New breeds of highly adaptable fishing kayaks and inflatables have now made it possible to fish the inshore zone for a much wider variety of species in areas that are virtually unreachable by land-based anglers.

One of the advantages of fishing Baja's inshore waters from a kayak or inflatable raft is having the ability to troll your bait or lure at a much slower speed than is usually possible in a motorized craft. Many surface fish, such as bonito and barracuda, prefer a lure that

Years before the onset of the kayak fishing craze in the mid-1990s, the author regularly fished successfully off of the Punta Banda peninsula from his small Sevylor raft. (BOBBY "TRI-CHAMP" GONZALEZ)

moves rapidly through the water. Other species, like the highly prized white sea bass, are more likely to inhale a live mackerel or lure that is pulled somewhat deeper at a slower speed.

The portability factor is also a big advantage if you visit regions that have no launch ramps or other facilities that allow easy access for larger, aluminum boats. New, state-of-the-art fabrics now being used by manufacturers of inflatable boats have added a dimension of safety and reliability that was nearly impossible to achieve only a few years ago.

While inflatables by Zodiak and Avon once dominated this market, other companies such as Sea Eagle and Sevylor have now become keen competitors, offering dependable inflatable fishing boats in the $150 to $300 range. For a little bit more, industry leaders such as Ocean Kayak offer several hard-bodied, sit-on-top kayaks that are perfect for inshore fishing at prices well under $1,000. My personal favorite is Ocean Kayak's Prowler Big Game series, which is extremely stable even for "plus-size" kayakers.

Don't be fooled into thinking that a fishing kayak is just an adult toy that is able to catch only smaller fish near shore. The striped marlin in the photo was one of nine that were caught on a trip in October 2005 with La Jolla Kayak Fishing from the Hotel Punta Colorada in the East Cape region of Baja. Owner/guide Jim Sammons's client, Dave

Kayaks can handle more than just small inshore species. This 160-pound striped marlin was caught by expert kayak guide Jim Sammons (left) and his client Dave Schlottman. (LA JOLLA KAYAK FISHING)

Schlottman, fought this 160-pound striped marlin for three hours in a spirited battle that covered more than 6 miles.

Other Useful Tools

Fish and Depth Finders

With today's digital technology, even small-craft and kayak anglers can now acquire effective electronic fish finders with many previously expensive features for a little over $100. Of course, the prices go up from there, but you can still get what you absolutely need for an affordable price. Even if you don't see any fish on the screen, always knowing your depth will help you to determine where drop-offs and high spots—which often hold fish—are located.

Various species tend to congregate along ledges, reefs, and underwater canyons that drop off into deeper water, which makes them a bit easier to locate by targeting those areas. Conversely, high spots where relatively small plateaus and pinnacles rise up abruptly from the depths are also good places to look for fish. This is particularly true in regard to migratory pelagic species, which are most prolific during the warmer months. Schools of offshore baitfish will usually encounter these high spots and be driven up toward the surface by ravenous predator species. Here, they may also be attacked from the air by hungry gulls, pelicans, and other birds, which also make them visible to alert anglers who happen to be in the same area.

Mounted or Handheld GPS Units

These days, there is practically no excuse for not incorporating one of these little gems into your equipment package for fishing in Baja, or just about anywhere else for that matter. Not only will having one help you to find previously established GPS waypoints and to easily mark productive fishing spots that you find on your own, but in the event of an emergency while you're out on the water having one aboard can literally save your life. When teamed with a VHF radio, or sometimes even a cell phone, it is just one extra insurance policy to help assure both your safety and angling success.

Fluorocarbon Leaders

In my opinion, one of the most revolutionary evolutions of fishing line in recent decades came with the introduction of fluorocarbon. Fluorocarbon, which is made by a variety of manufacturers, becomes practically invisible underwater and therefore allows anglers to use a heavier line to go after fish that might normally only be taken with ultralight line. Fluorocarbon is highly abrasion-resistant. Most anglers use fluorocarbon leaders that range between 18 to 28 inches in length, depending upon the species being targeted.

Scents Make Sense

The idea of adding some sort of special "essence" or fish attractant to an artificial lure in order to help fool a fish into inhaling it is certainly not a new concept—freshwater anglers have been using attractants for years. Recently, however, a new breed of attractant has appeared on the retail market, with many brands now targeted at saltwater anglers. Most of these contemporary concoctions incorporate special enzymes and oils to help provoke strikes, and seem to be particularly effective when used on plastic baits. Aside from those grubs and swimbaits that come already impregnated with some sort of scent, the majority of these types of products are applied topically to the lure itself.

My favorite way of accomplishing this task with the least amount of mess or waste is to simply place an appropriately sized dab of the selected product into a snack-size plastic "zip" bag along with a few of the plastics that I plan to use. I then roll them around inside the bag until each artificial bait is well covered. That way, one is always ready to be put onto a hook or leadhead jig at a moment's notice.

Over the years, there are a few brands that have become my personal favorites. They are: Hot Sauce, Smelly Jelly, Pro-Cure, and Uni Butter. Uni Butter is a rather new product made from sea urchin roe, a favored item in the diet of numerous inshore saltwater fishes almost everywhere that urchins are found.

Recommended Natural Baits

Anchovy (*Engraulis mordax*)

Except when fishing out of Ensenada on a private charter or a large commercial sport fishing vessel, most anglers in Baja waters usually never have a chance to fish with live anchovies. Nevertheless, depending upon their condition and the way they are rigged, frozen anchovies can work almost as well in many areas around the Baja peninsula. While plain anchovies look prettier in the freezer, the salted ones tend to be tougher and stay on the hook a bit better. Chopped-up anchovies also make excellent chum when your boat is at anchor, and you toss a few small chunks over your stern every few minutes.

Anchovies

Pacific Sardine (*Sardinops sagax*)

Once a staple species of commercial processors on Monterey Bay's Cannery Row, the Pacific sardine suddenly decided to disappear from the California coast in the early 1950s. Since then, they have come and gone, but when they are around, Pacific sardines are prime baitfish for catching a number of popular gamesters. Although you will generally not find them available as frozen bait, some fish markets on Baja's Pacific coast sell fresh ones that have been commercially harvested. Once again, the condition of the bait and the way it is rigged play an important role in how effective it will end up being.

Cortez Sardina (*Harengula thrissina*)

Not a true sardine, this flatiron herring is the staple live bait of the East Cape and the Sea of Cortez. They are generally netted by local fishermen early in the morning and then sold within a few hours to anglers who are headed out for the day on a chartered panga or cruiser. These baitfish do not come cheap and, depending upon how available they are at any given time, they can cost between $2 and $4 each. Left-over dead sardinas can sometimes be purchased for a lot less, but the Cortez sardina seems to catch a lot more fish when it is still alive.

Cortez sardina

Pacific Greenback Mackerel (*Scomber japonicus*)

This high-profile member of the mackerel family, sometimes called the chub mackerel, is commonly caught on Lucky Joe or Sabiki-style bait rigs. The best mackerel for bait are 6 to 11 inches in length, although you can use bigger ones if you happen to be targeting fish over 40 to 50 pounds. Larger mackerel can also be filleted and used as strip baits for a variety of species, and the cleaned carcasses can then be broken up and placed in a ventilated chum bucket for use as an effective fish attractant. Frozen mackerel can be either rigged whole or cut into chunk bait, but the fresh stuff usually catches a lot more fish.

Pacific greenback mackerel

Squid (*Loligo opalescens*)

Known to Southern California anglers as "candy bait" because it is so universally loved by gamefish, squid is at its very best when used

Squid

as bait while still alive. This can be hard to accomplish south of the border, because you will rarely find live squid available for sale in Baja. The only alternative is to try to catch a few at night using high-beam halogen lights and squid jigs, although these days those much larger Humboldt squid might try to horn in on the action as well.

Bringing along frozen blocks of squid on your Baja fishing trip provides you with a valuable insurance policy if there is little or no bait available when you reach your destination. Squid is one of the most versatile baits you can have; you can rig it whole with a stinger hook, cut it up and fish with chunks, or slice up strips to pin onto a jig or even on a bare hook. If you are lucky enough to catch some with a squid jig, be sure to throw a few immediately on ice if they should die in your bait tank. As a bonus, after cleaning and quickly frying them up you can reward yourself with a tasty treat that evening.

Mussels (*Mytilus californianus*)

These bivalves are the most plentiful yet underused bait resources on Baja's Pacific coast. Locals harvest them more for food than for fish bait, but they are also a favorite menu item for a long list of inshore species. One of the most difficult things about using them is getting the shelled, slippery mass to stay on the hook. Some anglers use orange

Mussels

thread to secure the mussel without the binding being too visible. But I prefer to simply cut them on the half shell and then set them face up in the sun for an hour or so. The membrane then dries up and gets tougher, making the mussels easier to bait up. The exposure to the sun also helps to ripen the mussels a bit, making them more aromatic for potential takers once you cast them out.

Ghost Shrimp (*Callianassa californiensis*)

Intertidal zones and esteros on the Pacific side of Baja are also home to the wily ghost shrimp. Evidence of its presence are small, occasionally mounded, holes in the sand that are usually found well below the normal tidal mark. Casual observers might first believe that these are clam holes and, indeed, some might also harbor razor or pencil clams; but most of them were actually dug by ghost shrimp. When properly rigged and presented, ghost shrimp can be one of the most consistently deadly baits for spotfin and yellowfin croaker, sargo, spotted bay bass, sand bass, corbina, flounder, and halibut, as well as for a wide variety of perch species.

Ghost shrimp range in color between white, pale pink, and bright

Ghost shrimp

orange, with males possessing one claw that is much larger than that of the females. They have few natural predators except for birds, fish, and anglers, who take them from their burrows to use as bait. You can try to dig them up with a shovel, but the 3-foot PVC suction pumps available at certain bait and tackle stores work much better.

Because of their somewhat soft bodies and overall physical structure, ghost shrimp require a specific type of hooking technique for optimum effectiveness. A wide-gap hook, No. 2 to No. 4 is ideal, although sizes up to No. 2/0 may be needed for larger shrimp. No matter the hook size, it is vital to thread the ghost shrimp gently onto the hook so that it maintains a normal appearance, and then cast it very carefully so that it doesn't fly off the hook.

Recommended Artificial Baits

NOTE: None of the following brand suggestions represents a paid endorsement; each recommendation is merely my own personal preference for fishing the waters of Baja California.

Plastic Baits—Onshore, Inshore, and Offshore

Mann's is a longtime player in the freshwater market, but their small plastic grubs are also deadly when pursuing fish in Baja's many saltwater esteros and surf zones.

Kalin is a trusted brand of plastic tails that have proven to be effective in catching many of Baja's inshore species. Their double-tailed Scampi has been an angler's favorite for decades.

Swimbaits

Use leadhead jigs weighing between $\frac{1}{4}$ ounce and 3 ounces on 3- to 8-inch swimbaits. Fish Trap Lures makes popular plastics that come in a variety of colors and feature a lifelike action that is known for triggering strikes around the Baja Peninsula.

Relatively new on the market, MC Swimbaits are sluglike jerk baits and drop-shot plastics that are absolutely deadly, particularly on halibut and other inshore species.

Spoons—Inshore and Offshore

The Luhr Jensen Krocodile has been an old standby of veteran Baja anglers for many decades. It is virtually irresistible when cast near a school of active gamefish. The Luhr Jensen Crippled Herring is a newer variation on the classic spoon design that has proven effective on many saltwater species common to Baja California waters.

The Hopkins Spoon, available in both silver and golden hues, is of traditional, durable construction that makes it an all-time favorite in Baja.

Saltwater Flies—Inshore and Offshore

The Lefty's Deceiver fly pattern is one that regularly fools numerous Baja gamefish. Tie your own in different sizes and colors to imitate a wide variety of baitfish species, or buy them from Orvis and other fly tackle retailers.

Hard Baits—Inshore and Offshore

Rebel Lures makes a wide variety of both standard and jointed plugs that have been favored in Baja for decades. The Rapala is a Scandinavian classic that has long proven to be deadly on a wide variety of Baja gamefish.

Braid is a highly respected brand of hard baits among Baja anglers. Dennis Braid's new Viper has a lifelike, double-jointed action that offers a provocative new concept in swimming plugs.

Yo-Zuri Japanese lures are also gaining a reputation in Baja for catching everything from tuna and dorado to wahoo and marlin.

Iron Lures—Inshore and Offshore

Salas "irons" were among the first, and are still some of the best for fishing the waters of Baja California. Tady is one of the most respected brands for both surface and bottom iron, and remains near the top of the list for Baja anglers.

Sumo is relative newcomer to the marketplace, but is rapidly becoming a preferred iron bait for fishing off the Baja peninsula. Action-Lures live up to their name; with a unique jointed design that works well in Baja to provoke strikes at any depth.

Jethead Skirts—Offshore

Sevenstrand is one of the original companies to feature a jethead design, which is a perfect format for trolling plastic skirts in Baja. Zuker jetheads also have a longstanding reputation as one of Baja's most deadly tools when trolling for big gamefish offshore.

Prepackaged Fishing Adventures at Baja's East Cape Resorts

More than a half century ago, the legendary writer, angler, and Baja aficionado Ray Cannon fell in love with the East Cape region and professed the waters of the Sea of Cortez to be a "giant fish trap." Since then, literally millions of anglers have visited the East Cape and returned home to confirm Cannon's enthusiastic portrayal of the area.

The East Cape of Baja California Sur features a style of fishing resort
that is uniquely different from those found elsewhere on the peninsula.
(RICK ROESSLER)

For those who would still like to experience some of Baja's hot fishing action, but would rather not bother with the trouble and expense of pulling down their own craft, the East Cape region of Baja Sur offers a particularly unique type of accommodations for the avid angler. These hotels feature in-house fishing fleets, fish processing services, and lodging plans that include three meals a day, and will even supply box lunches for anglers who will be out on the water at lunchtime. This environment has been created with the comfort of the angler in mind, and caters to their sometimes obsessive desire to immerse themselves in all things involving fishing for several days at a time. The major players in this highly specialized arena are profiled below.

Buena Vista Hotel and Beach Resort

Don't be fooled by the Hotel Buena Vista's extensive tropical land-scaping, luxury suites, and "swim-up" cocktail bar. Fishing is still the primary drawing card for the many guests who regularly flock to the Hotel Buena Vista Beach Resort, which is situated between San José del Cabo and La Paz near the tip of the Baja peninsula. It is also a beau-tiful oasis that is fed by pristine natural hot springs, and provides a per-fect setting to enjoy its colorful floral scenery in unabashed relaxation.

In 1981, Jesus "Chuy" Valdez, a young entrepreneur with great vi-sions for the future, purchased the property during an era when the East Cape was virtually undiscovered. He quickly began expanding the hotel to include 60 rooms, a fleet of 20 fishing boats, a swimming pool, lushly landscaped grounds, and a world-class restaurant.

Over the years, Valdez, along with his sons Axel, Felipe, and the rest of the family, have worked diligently to turn the property into what it is today, a first-rate fishing resort that can hold its own when compared to its counterparts anywhere else in the world.

Rancho Leonero

Rancho Leonero is located on a small point, which allows it to take advantage of the prevailing coastal breezes. Directly in front of the hotel, a double reef of boulders provides habitat for a wide variety of fishes that will delight both the snorkeler and the inshore angler. Without a doubt, if there is such a thing as a spiritual vortex on our planet, this is one of them.

Despite its bucolic atmosphere, the ranch still manages to run like a well-maintained Rolex, with a great deal of credit going to the efforts of Gary Barnes Webb. This transplanted South African possesses a broad spectrum of talents that have allowed him to efficiently address a bevy of ongoing infrastructure- and staff-related issues, while deftly coordinating the ranch's sport fishing fleet of pangas and cruisers.

Although the nearby sandy beaches, inviting hammocks, pool, and on-site massages may encourage guests to relax, it is hard to deny that one of the primary activities at Rancho Leonero is fishing. There is something here for every type of angler. Fly-fishing expert Jeff de Brown offers his clients at the ranch one of the few Orvis-certified guide services on the Baja Peninsula, and sees to it that they are able to take full advantage of this world-famous venue for angling with the fly.

The kayak fishing in this region is exceptional. And, as one of the southland's initial developers and promoters of this popular sport, Dennis Spike consistently proves himself to be uniquely qualified to put experienced anglers on the bite, while patiently instructing and encouraging someone who may be fishing from a kayak for the very first time.

There is even something here for the shore angler, particularly during the dark of night! Those who are willing to toss out a well-rigged mullet or ladyfish near the dock during an evening high tide are sometimes rewarded with large pargo and snapper capable of burning out their drag washers.

One thing is certain: travelers with a love for hot, rod-bending action on the water will have to go a long way to find a more appropriate or affordable destination than the East Cape of Baja Sur. It is a magical region, and few have been able to better convey and uphold the true spirit of "old Baja" than John Ireland and his capable staff at Rancho Leonero.

Punta Colorada—Van Wormer Resorts

The Hotel Punta Colorada is situated on a sandy point at the southern end of the East Cape. Over the years it has gained a well-earned reputation as the "roosterfish capital of the world."

With its miles of untouched white sand beach that offers superb fishing, swimming, snorkeling, and scuba diving, the hotel remains one of the few first-class fishing resorts that punctuate Baja's coastal wilderness. The resorts on Baja Sur's East Cape are a world apart from the sometimes gaudy commercialization of Mexico's more urban hotel properties.

The Van Wormer family pioneered the establishment of this type of East Cape resort, and they also own and manage the popular nearby tourist resorts of Playa Del Sol and Hotel Palmas de Cortez.

Baja Fishing Maps

WARNING: Fishing map text corresponds with GPS charts #1 through #16. The information contained within these maps is intended solely as a guide for anglers to use as starting points in their quest to find fish. None of these fishing charts, nor any datum contained therein, is meant in any way to be used as a navigation tool or related resource of any kind. Mariners are strongly encouraged to maintain constant vigilance in regard to weather conditions, currents, and potential navigational hazards at all times while boating, fishing, or sailing on the inshore, coastal, or offshore waters surrounding the Baja California peninsula.

Map 1—Islas Los Coronados

Located just below the border, barely 18 miles southwest of San Diego, the Coronado Islands are the closest fishing venue in Baja for United States anglers who are targeting traditional summer favorites such as yellowtail, bonito, white sea bass, and occasionally, even bluefin or yellowfin tuna. During the winter months, action on the bottom for lingcod, rockfish, and other deepwater denizens is the primary draw for passengers who are willing to brave sometimes choppy seas and chilly gusts in order to fill up the burlap bags hanging near the bait tank.

Since the enactment of numerous federal regulations forbidding the take of various rockfish species within US waters during the winter, Baja California has become one of the few winter resources for anglers in search of these tasty fish, which are often listed on restaurant menus as Pacific red snapper.

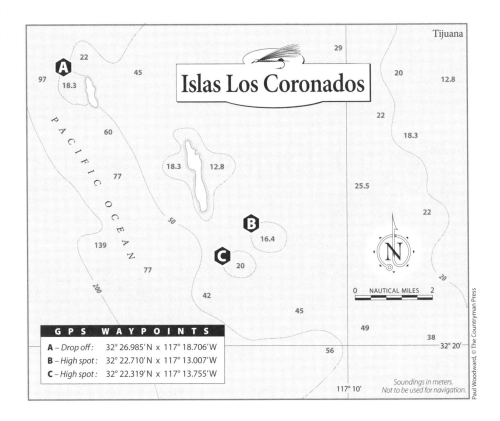

Islas Los Coronados

Tijuana

PACIFIC OCEAN

97   22
18.3   45
60   29   20   12.8
77   22
18.3   12.8   18.3
50   25.5
139   16.4   22
77   20
200   42   20
45   49   38   32° 20'
56   32° 20'

0   NAUTICAL MILES   2

Paul Woodward, © The Countryman Press

Soundings in meters.
Not to be used for navigation.

117° 10'

G P S   W A Y P O I N T S

A – *Drop off :*   32° 26.985′ N x 117° 18.706′ W
B – *High spot :*   32° 22.710′ N x 117° 13.007′ W
C – *High spot :*   32° 22.319′ N x 117° 13.755′ W

For those fishing Islas Los Coronados from one of the commercial sport fishers based in southern California, live bait is plentiful and the crew is likely to chum the water nearby, particularly while fishing for surface species, in order to keep the bends in their customers' fishing rods. But anglers fishing from private craft must be more judicious with their limited bait supply, and will often troll Rapala-style lures in patterns that resemble mackerel, sardines, or similar baitfish at 6 to 9 knots near the islands and outcroppings, or under working birds. Once a hook-up occurs, live baits can then be quickly cast out to attract other predatory fish that may also be swimming in the area.

In early spring, when the water is still relatively cold, the first yellowtail of the season are often caught at depths of 80 to 150 feet. These are the times when heavier metal jigs can easily outfish live bait, which is harder to get down in a presentable manner and still provide the action necessary to provoke a strike.

Although many of those who fish the Coronado Islands focus on catching the local favorites, there are still others who prefer drifting over the sandy bottom on the lee side of the southern island with a live, trap-rigged sardine or mackerel. They are in search of large California halibut that lay intermittently camouflaged by sand while waiting patiently for an unsuspecting victim to swim by.

Several International Game Fish Association (IGFA) line-class world record halibut have been taken in this area, which is situated at the northern tip of a region known as the "halibut triangle." On July 3, 1994, Shirley Blackman, wife of renowned boat manufacturer Don Blackman, set one record with her huge, 41-pound California halibut caught on 16-pound-test monofilament line—that record that is still on the books.

Map 2—Ensenada/Bahía de Todos Santos

The Mediterranean-like seaport of Ensenada lies less than 100 miles south of the international border at San Ysidro and is situated adjacent to a large, natural harbor known as Bahía de Todos Santos. In the late 1940s and 1950s, Ensenada earned the nickname "yellowtail capital

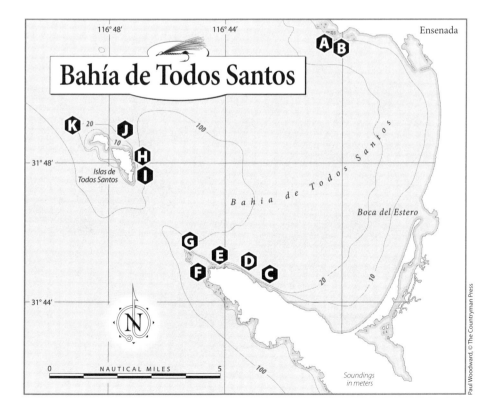

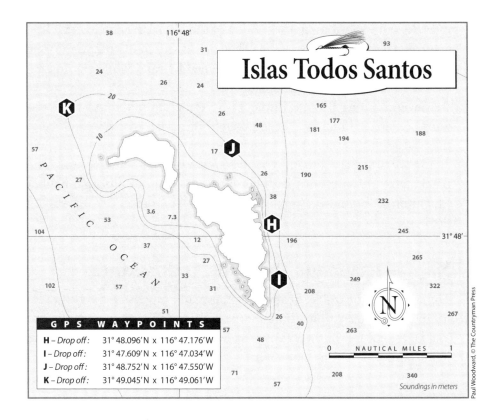

Islas Todos Santos

GPS WAYPOINTS

H – Drop off : 31° 48.096′ N x 116° 47.176′ W
I – Drop off : 31° 47.609′ N x 116° 47.034′ W
J – Drop off : 31° 48.752′ N x 116° 47.550′ W
K – Drop off : 31° 49.045′ N x 116° 49.061′ W

Soundings in meters

Paul Woodward, © The Countryman Press

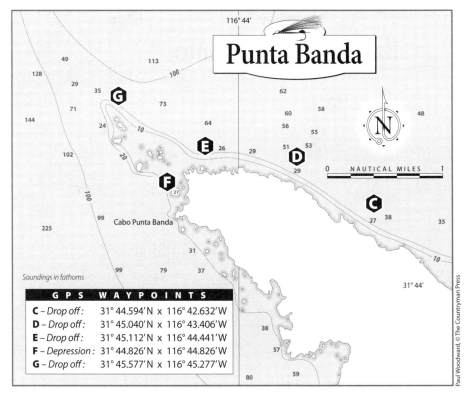

Punta Banda

Cabo Punta Banda

Soundings in fathoms

GPS WAYPOINTS

C – Drop off : 31° 44.594′ N x 116° 42.632′ W
D – Drop off : 31° 45.040′ N x 116° 43.406′ W
E – Drop off : 31° 45.112′ N x 116° 44.441′ W
F – Depression : 31° 44.826′ N x 116° 44.826′ W
G – Drop off : 31° 45.577′ N x 116° 45.277′ W

Paul Woodward, © The Countryman Press

of the world," which was verified by countless photographs of happy anglers holding up large stringers filled to capacity with this hard-fighting cousin of the amberjack.

Population growth and commercial development, along with such practices as overharvesting and bait seining, have had some impact over the years. But Ensenada Bay remains a productive fishery that supports year-round action with a wide variety of species.

The bay offers miles of unobstructed sandy beach just south of the city that features excellent fishing for halibut, barred surf perch, corbina, and sand bass, as well as for both yellowfin and spotfin croaker. The nearby kelp beds also offer exceptional action for barracuda, yellowtail, bonito, and calico bass. Las Islas Todos Santos lie about 8 miles offshore, and provide habitat for numerous species of popular gamefish, including a host of bottom dwellers such as lingcod and rockfish in the *Sebastes* family. For those seeking bigger quarry, the rocky outcroppings near La Bufadora and the tip of at the southern end of the bay offer an opportunity to hook up with a large yellowtail or trophy white sea bass. As an added bonus, tuna species such as albacore, yellowfin, bigeye, and bluefin are usually available offshore during late summer and fall.

There are a number of commercial sport fishing vessels available near the public fish market along Ensenada's seawall that take passengers out on trips to various locations on a year-round basis. For those who trailer down their own boats, the Coral Hotel and Marina near Punta Morro just north of town is the premier resort property of its kind in the Ensenada area. Several of the sandy spots just outside its rocky jetty and breakwater can provide a great seasonal halibut bite for anglers who can resist the temptation of venturing into deeper waters. Try fishing on the drift using trap-rigged anchovies or sardines, either live or dead. Swimbaits and other plastics are also productive, but natural baits seem to have an edge here.

Bahía de Todos Santos ends at the southerly point where a long sand beach meets the massive, hill-covered peninsula of Punta Banda, which juts out into the Pacific Ocean. This usually causes the beach break in that area to be quite small, allowing for the shore launching of smaller aluminum craft, inflatables, and pangas from a professional sport fishing charter service nearby to take advantage of some of the excellent angling opportunities to be found in this area. Those who choose to fish this spot from their own craft should start by working the area past the sand beach and along the cliffs, about 150 yards to

0.25 mile from shore, using plastic swimbaits or anchovies drifted across the bottom. When a particularly active bite is located, move periodically back upwind or upcurrent, and keep repeating the drift until there is no more action in the area. Expect to catch sand bass, calico bass, halibut, small rockfish, and an occasional yellowtail.

Near the tip of Punta Banda, the water gets much deeper and sits in the path of a coldwater current originating in the Gulf of Alaska. As you approach the end of the point, numerous guano-covered outcroppings composed of ancient lava deposits come into view. Fish the intermittently rocky bottom spots near this area with live bait and lures for anything from lingcod to white sea bass. Work around as many of the lava outcroppings as possible, but remain constantly aware of changing wind and current conditions, as they can be navigational hazards. During the late spring and summer months, this area provides excellent fishing for surface species such as yellowtail, bonito, and barracuda. At other times, sending a dropper loop rig baited with squid, anchovies, or sardines to the bottom may result in a rockfish or sand bass.

Map 3—Puerto Santo Tomás

As the crow flies, Puerto Santo Tomás is only a few miles south of the tip of Punta Banda. But to access it via a land route from there could easily take you a few hours, depending upon road conditions. Occasionally, commercial sport fishing boats from Ensenada will make the trip down to Santo Tomás Reef, but these waters are generally fished only by the local panga fleet and private sportfishers from more northerly ports.

To reach Puerto Santo Tomás From the Ensenada area, take the main highway south. After passing through the small town of Maneadero, continue driving south for approximately 15 miles. You may encounter a military checkpoint along the way, but you can relax—harassing tourists and anglers is not part of the soldiers' assignment.

A mile or so beyond this point, the winding road descends down into the Santo Tomás Valley. Between kilometer markers 46 and 47, you will see a sign on the right that reads PUERTO SANTO TOMÁS. Proceed approximately 150 feet past the road sign and make a right turn onto the gravel road that heads west, and continue on for about 18 miles, making sure to always bear to the right when you come to intermittent forks in the road.

When you reach the coast and the humble poblado of La Bocana, veer to your right and climb the small hill as you head north. Continue along this sparsely maintained coastal pathway for approximately 3 more miles until you reach the protected cove at the very end.

Puerto Santo Tomás Resort is perched just above this bucolic grotto, which embodies the spirit of the "old Baja" that existed before many regions of the peninsula were commercially developed to their present state. While rooms and the related amenities at the resort are readily available, this is also a fantastic area to visit for those who appreciate "dry camping" in a picturesque, primitive environment that offers unparalleled opportunities for onshore, inshore, and offshore fishing as well as excellent kayaking, hiking, and beachcombing.

Pangas are available for hire, but this is also a prime location for fishing from a kayak, cartop aluminum boat, or inflatable. Try working around the edges of nearby kelp beds. Slowly trolling lures or live baits in these spots during the midsummer months is a deadly method for taking bonito, calico bass, barracuda, yellowtail, and white sea bass. Nearshore drop-offs to deeper water allow anglers to lower heavier iron lures or baited, multiple-hook gangions down to a host of

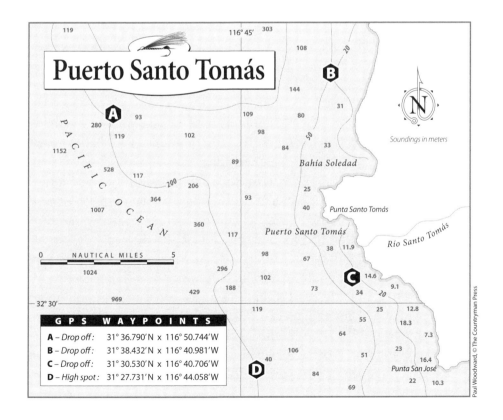

GPS WAYPOINTS		
A – Drop off:	31° 36.790'N x 116° 50.744'W
B – Drop off:	31° 38.432'N x 116° 40.981'W
C – Drop off:	31° 30.530'N x 116° 40.706'W
D – High spot:	31° 27.731'N x 116° 44.058'W

Paul Woodward, © The Countryman Press

hungry rockfish, lingcod, and red rock cod.

Puerto Santo Tomás also happens to be one of the most accessible primitive shore fishing locations for anglers visiting from north of the border. I always suggest that visitors who plan to fish in Baja bring along at least one 5-pound block of frozen squid to use as bait. Plastic lures, spoons, and sometimes even iron jigs can be productive while fishing onshore. But what most of the local inshore species are really hungry for is clinging tenaciously to the rocks at your very feet, and can be easily harvested at low tide. Fresh Pacific black mussels are not only tasty when cooked in a variety of ways, but are also one of the best baits available for those fishing from the rocky Pacific coastline of Baja California Norte.

Map 4—Bahía San Quintin

Over the decades, Bahía San Quintin has become one of the top summertime sport fishing destinations on Baja's Pacific coast. Offshore, pelagic species such as dorado, albacore, and yellowfin and bluefin tuna are seasonal favorites, along with bonito, barracuda, sand bass, and yellowtail. During cooler months, nearby San Martin Island offers great fishing for large rockfish and lingcod, while the area outside the mouth of Bahía San Quintin is noted for producing California halibut over 25 pounds and an occasional giant black sea bass. Just a few miles to the south, the inshore waters off El Socorro Beach can yield quality white sea bass up to almost 70 pounds.

There is also excellent clamming and beachcombing available along San Quintin's many miles of sandy shoreline. The shallow back bays are a sanctuary for the southerly migration of thousands of black brant that annually join the native quail population to create a bird hunter's paradise. These waters are also home to one of the most prolific aquaculture industries on the entire Baja peninsula, which produces tons of fresh oysters, clams, and mussels each year.

The north end of the bay offers food, lodging, a small dirt airstrip, and sport fishing services, which include trips on both pangas for inshore fishing, and 20- to 30-foot cruisers for those with a mind to go fishing offshore. Smart anglers will bring along several Lucky Joe–style bait rigs to use near the mouth of the bay to load up on small live mackerel for bait. No matter where you plan to fish or what you plan to target, there are very few predatory species in this area that will turn down a young, lively mackerel that is properly rigged and presented.

Although the mainstay of the year-round commercial and recre-

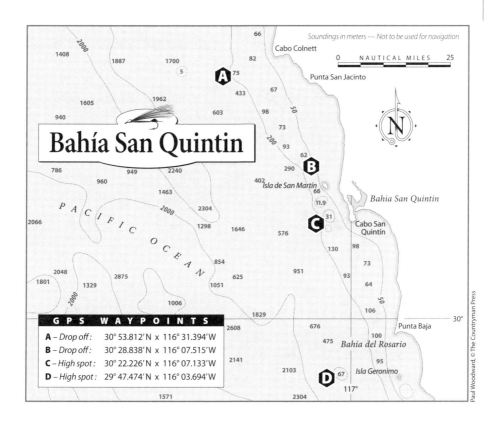

Soundings in meters — Not to be used for navigation

Cabo Colnett

Punta San Jacinto

0   NAUTICAL MILES   25

N

Bahía San Quintin

Isla de San Martín

Bahia San Quintin

Cabo San Quintín

PACIFIC OCEAN

Punta Baja   30°

Bahía del Rosario

Isla Geronimo

117°

Paul Woodward, © The Countryman Press

G P S   W A Y P O I N T S

A – Drop off :   30° 53.812′N x 116° 31.394′W
B – Drop off :   30° 28.838′N x 116° 07.515′W
C – High spot :   30° 22.226′N x 116° 07.133′W
D – High spot :   29° 47.474′N x 116° 03.694′W

ational fishermen here may be the quality-grade lingcod and red rock cod that are so prolific in the region, the offshore action for big, pelagic yellowtail and various members of the tuna family during the late summer and early fall draws anglers from all over the map.

Sadly, a few high-tech, aircraft-equipped commercial fishing interests have been spotting and wrapping large schools of these valuable gamefish in their purse seine nets over the past few years almost as fast as they have appeared offshore. Luckily for anglers, one local outfitter, K&M Sportfishing, has a fleet of several Parker cruisers that they use to quickly spirit their clients out to take advantage of the bite before the commercial boats even have an opportunity to reach the area and set up their nets. As you can imagine, a lively and sometimes hostile verbal exchange can take place when these two contingents collide but, fortunately, anything beyond that rarely occurs.

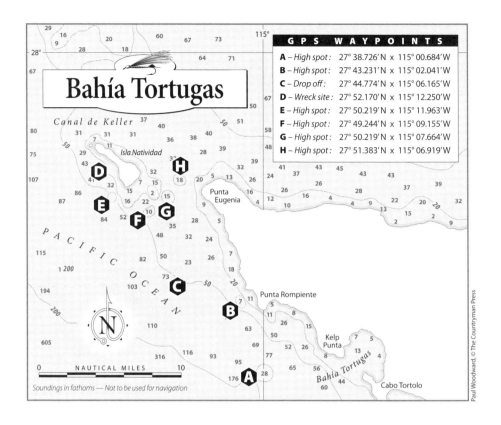

Map 5—Bahía Tortugas

Although remote, the launch ramp at Bahía Tortugas offers one of the better such access points along Baja's rural Pacific coast for trailer boat anglers. This fact is primarily due to the highly active commercial fishing interests in the area.

Once launched, the small craft or kayak angler will find a number of good fishing spots within the bay itself. The inshore waters along the salty shoreline well south of the launch ramp is a great area to fish for halibut between May and October, and is also a good place to make mackerel bait with a Lucky Joe or Sabiki rig prior to heading outside to fish.

The mouth of Bahía Tortugas is protected by heavy kelp beds, which also offer excellent summertime fishing for the famous "three Bs" of Southern California: bass, barracuda, and bonito. This is also a reliable area for marauding yellowtail during the summer.

For larger craft, there are a number of high spots and drop-offs that span the offshore waters just to the northwest of the bay. They offer solid bottom action for numerous species during the colder months, and also create a focal point for rising schools of baitfish in the summer, which in turn draw pelagic gamefish such as dorado and tuna to those areas as well.

Map 6—Bahía Asunción

Even more remote than Bahía Tortugas, the more southerly Bahía Asunción can be a great place to get your line wet, even though it may take you a little more time and effort to get there. As in Bahía Tortugas just to the north, the incomes of most of the residents are supported by the commercial harvest and canning of seafood products taken from the rich waters nearby, perhaps the most prominent of these being abalone.

For the recreational angler, Bahía Asunción presents a number of venues for great inshore fishing. If you happen to be a kayak angler with a love of calico bass, you may think that you have died and gone to heaven after fishing for them here. The calicos are not only plentiful, they are *big!* A 10-pound fish that would be viewed as an incredible catch in Southern California is fairly commonplace in this neck of the

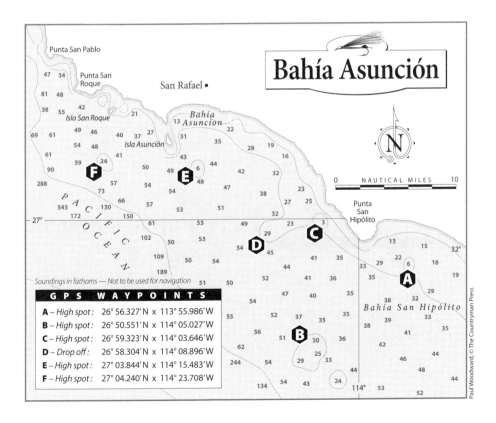

GPS WAYPOINTS

A – High spot: 26° 56.327′N x 113° 55.986′W
B – High spot: 26° 50.551′N x 114° 05.027′W
C – High spot: 26° 59.323′N x 114° 03.646′W
D – Drop off: 26° 58.304′N x 114° 08.896′W
E – High spot: 27° 03.844′N x 114° 15.483′W
F – High spot: 27° 04.240′N x 114° 23.708′W

Soundings in fathoms — Not to be used for navigation

Paul Woodward, © The Countryman Press

woods. Those who enjoy tossing plastics will have a field day, particularly between July and September.

Just a mile off the point, Isla Asunción offers exceptional structure for drawing in yellowtail, bonito, and barracuda. During late summer and fall, anglers can even catch a few of the dorado that occasionally breeze through.

Offshore, deeper drop-offs as well as several reefs and high spots offer places to search out working birds for tuna, dorado, and even marlin when the timing is right.

Map 7—Punta Abreojos

The Punta Abreojos region provides a plethora of fishing opportunities within close range of one another. Just off the actual point, there is great seasonal fishing for calico bass, leopard grouper, and yellowtail. Along the sandy surf zone just to the north, you will find what is arguably some of the best surf fishing to be had anywhere on Baja's Pacific coast. At the northern end of that beach, the mouth of Laguna La Bocana beckons anglers to fish its inner waters for abundant catches of

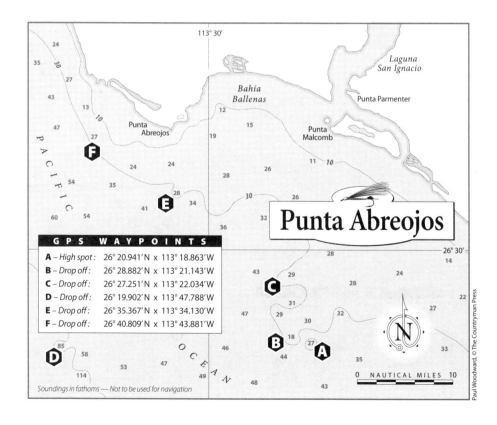

GPS WAYPOINTS

A – *High spot :* 26° 20.941′ N x 113° 18.863′ W
B – *Drop off :* 26° 28.882′ N x 113° 21.143′ W
C – *Drop off :* 26° 27.251′ N x 113° 22.034′ W
D – *Drop off :* 26° 19.902′ N x 113° 47.788′ W
E – *Drop off :* 26° 35.367′ N x 113° 34.130′ W
F – *Drop off :* 26° 40.809′ N x 113° 43.881′ W

Soundings in fathoms — Not to be used for navigation

Paul Woodward, © The Countryman Press

leopard grouper, shortfin corbina, and the ubiquitous spotted bay bass.

Offshore, there is spirited action for pelagic species like tuna and dorado, as well as a number of drop-offs and rocky depressions that host various members of the grouper family, a few of which can weigh upwards of several hundred pounds.

As if that is not already enough, a bit farther down the curving coastline sits the enchanting Estero de Coyote and Rene's Camp, which offers primitive camping, modest cabins, a decent restaurant, and a launch ramp. Depending upon tides and weather conditions, the fishing here can be excellent for spotted bay bass, corbina, small leopard grouper, and occasional halibut. It is, however, a unique ecosystem that is particularly impacted by low tidal ebbs that can literally leave many areas of the estero high and dry.

Map 8—Bahía Magdalena

The cloistered canals at Bahía Magdalena's northern end are a kayaker's dream, as well as a prime destination for avid fly anglers targeting the

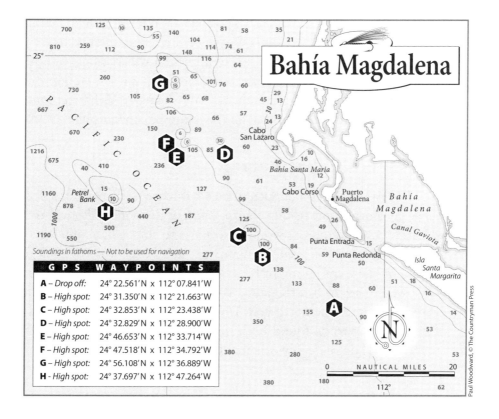

coveted robalo, known to Norte Americanos as snook. These mangroves are both a blessing and a menace, since they harbor many lurking cabrilla and grouper that are receptive to a fly or a lure, but are almost impossible to extricate from their nestlike roots once the fish are hooked.

For shore casters, the sandy bottom and calmer waters inside the bahía create a nearly perfect breeding ground for halibut. Although a live, trap-rigged smelt is one of the most dependable offerings for these highly prized flatties, shiny Krocodile-style spoons, swimbaits, or drop-shot plastics can be equally deadly. The summer months are a good time to catch corbina and spotted bay bass, a variety that is so profuse in some sections of the bay that it is practically considered a pest by those fishing for other species.

This incredibly diverse fishery with its assortment of inshore habitats can be accessed from ocean waters by several passes that run between the guardian islands, each of which can produce its own fair share of rod-bending action during tidal swings. The most successful anglers who fish these areas always keep an eye out for working birds or fleeing schools of surfacing baitfish as an indication of where to cast.

For those who choose to venture offshore, the summer and fall months can offer some of the most spectacular fishing available along the entire Pacific coast of Baja. These waters are blessed with numerous banks, pinnacles, and high spots that invite hungry gamesters like big yellowfin tuna, wahoo, and billfish to approach within range of both private and commercial craft. Between October and December, this area has been described by a number of billfish anglers as having some of the best striped marlin fishing on the entire Baja peninsula.

Map 9—Los Cabos Region

To be honest, unless you happen to be a hardcore party person, a passenger on a local sport fishing charter boat, or the potential buyer of a timeshare condominium, I would direct you to somewhere other than Cabo San Lucas if you are looking for a taste of the "true Baja."

The only exception might be if you happen to be bringing down your own cruiser to fish the Jaime Bank or Golden Gate Bank on the Pacific side just to the northwest. Don't get me wrong, there is plenty of good fishing to be found both inshore and offshore. It's just too crowded and commercially oriented for my own personal taste.

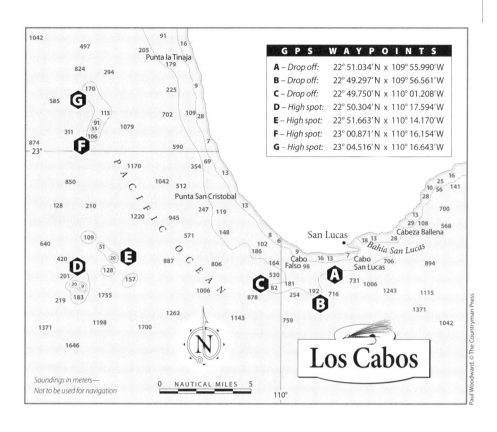

GPS WAYPOINTS

A – Drop off:	22° 51.034′N x 109° 55.990′W
B – Drop off:	22° 49.297′N x 109° 56.561′W
C – Drop off:	22° 49.750′N x 110° 01.208′W
D – High spot:	22° 50.304′N x 110° 17.594′W
E – High spot:	22° 51.663′N x 110° 14.170′W
F – High spot:	23° 00.871′N x 110° 16.154′W
G – High spot:	23° 04.516′N x 110° 16.643′W

Los Cabos

Soundings in meters—
Not to be used for navigation

0 NAUTICAL MILES 5

Paul Woodward, © The Countryman Press

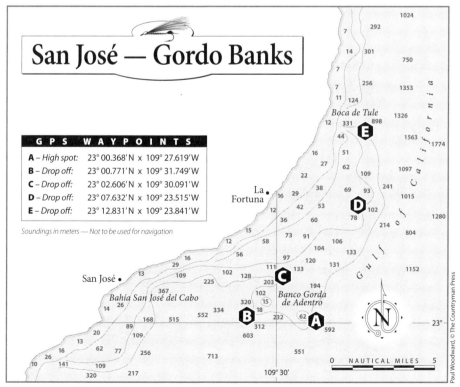

San José — Gordo Banks

GPS WAYPOINTS

A – High spot:	23° 00.368′N x 109° 27.619′W
B – Drop off:	23° 00.771′N x 109° 31.749′W
C – Drop off:	23° 02.606′N x 109° 30.091′W
D – Drop off:	23° 07.632′N x 109° 23.515′W
E – Drop off:	23° 12.831′N x 109° 23.841′W

Soundings in meters — Not to be used for navigation

0 NAUTICAL MILES 5

Paul Woodward, © The Countryman Press

Map 10—San José del Cabo

Although located only a few miles away from Cabo San Lucas, the more muted town of San José also offers good inshore fishing as well as some great offshore action at the famous Gordo Banks nearby. During certain times of the year, boats out of Puerto San Lucas will even go all the way over to the Cortez side of the cape to take advantage of more seasonally productive fishing for species like dorado, marlin, and wahoo.

Several miles up the coast, the famed East Cape fishing resorts near Los Barriles offer customized accommodations for anglers. Most of the hotels in this area feature multiple-day packages that include lodging, meals, and either panga or cruiser charter service to most of the local hotspots, from the Gordo Banks in the south all the way up to Cerralvo Island, which lies just north of Cabo.

Map 11—Cerralvo Island/Las Arenas

Situated between the East Cape and Baja Sur's capital city of La Paz, the waters between the tip of Punta Arenas and the southern end of Cer-

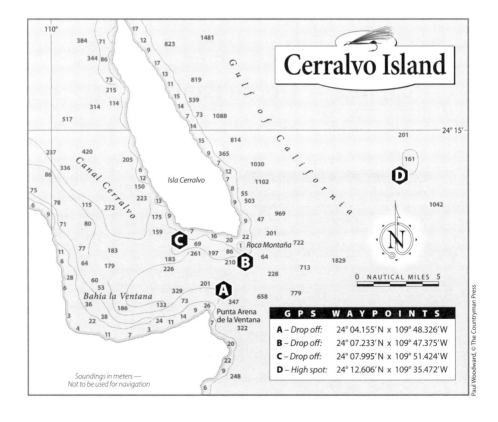

Barrel cactus

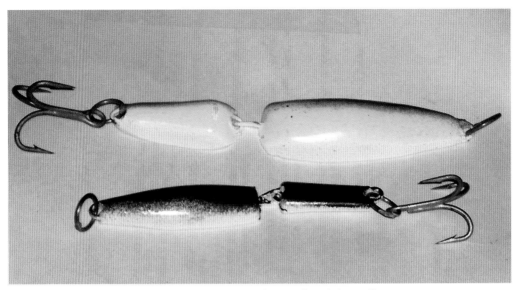

The jointed Action-Lure is one 'iron' that offers
lifelike movement, even at great depths. (TOM GATCH)

Sumo Tackle, a relative newcomer, is rapidly becoming a preferred brand
of iron bait among Baja anglers. (SUMO TACKLE)

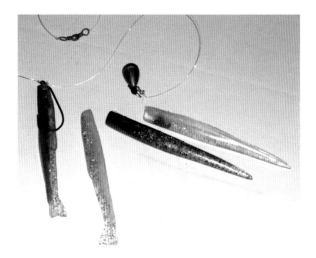

Relatively new on the market, the sluglike jerkbaits and drop-shot plastics from MC Swimbaits are absolutely deadly, particularly on halibut and other inshore species. (TOM GATCH)

The new Viper from Braid Products has a lifelike, double-jointed action that offers a provocative new concept in hard baits. (BRAID PRODUCTS)

Jonathan "Bluewater Jon" Schwartz in his element with
a fresh load of big yellowtail that he caught from his kayak off
of Bahía San Quintin. (JONATHAN SCHWARTZ)

The morning sun breaks over the Sea of Cortez with the promise of another great day on the water. (LYNN GATCH)

Capt. Ivan Villarino, owner of the Vonny's Fleet panga camp
in Punta Banda, vigilantly patrols the productive waters just beyond the tip
of the peninsula. (YVONNE VILLARINO)

A pirate indeed—at least to
the fish—Tailhunter International's
owner and guide Jonathan Roldan
abandoned Southern California's
crowded freeways for the
turquoise waters of La Paz years
ago, and has never regretted it.
(TAILHUNTER INTERNATIONAL)

Kayak fishing guru Dennis Spike heads out for another day of rod-bending action less than a mile off Rancho Leonero, one of the East Cape's premier angling resorts. (LYNN GATCH)

Expert Baja fly angler Gary Graham displays one of Baja's rare robalo (snook) taken on a fly in Magdalena Bay's inner estero. (GARY GRAHAM)

Homes with stunning coastal views may not
be cheap anywhere, but they are far more affordable along
the Baja California coast. (LYNN GATCH)

ralvo Island can serve up some of the most spectacular fishing in the entire region.

During late summer, schools of fat yellowfin tuna occasionally cruise so close to shore at Punta Arenas that they can sometimes be reached by long-distance shore casters throwing heavy iron jigs. Also in late summer, the hot sandy beaches to the south can play host to even hotter action for the big roosterfish that often patrol the waters within only 100 yards or less from shore.

Offshore, the tip of Cerralvo Island is a gathering point for tuna, marlin, and wahoo in summer, while the rocky structure at the bottom provides a home for the huge pargo and grouper that are a viable target for anglers during their active, early winter spawns.

Map 12—La Paz

La Paz is a pearl. In addition to being, in my opinion, the most beautiful city on the Baja Peninsula, the waters offshore are absolutely teeming with fish. While there is solid inshore fishing for smaller snapper, pargo, leopard grouper, and sierra, the offshore fishing really

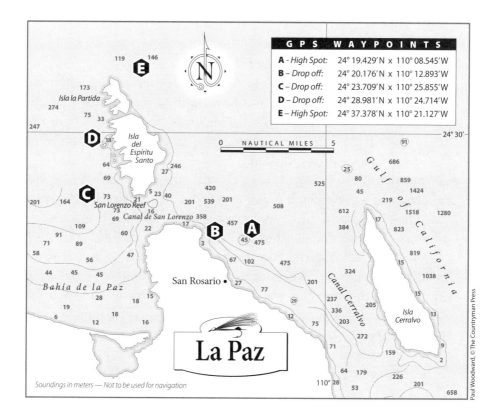

GPS WAYPOINTS	
A – High Spot:	24° 19.429′ N x 110° 08.545′ W
B – Drop off:	24° 20.176′ N x 110° 12.893′ W
C – Drop off:	24° 23.709′ N x 110° 25.855′ W
D – Drop off:	24° 28.981′ N x 110° 24.714′ W
E – High Spot:	24° 37.378′ N x 110° 21.127′ W

Soundings in meters — Not to be used for navigation

Paul Woodward, © The Countryman Press

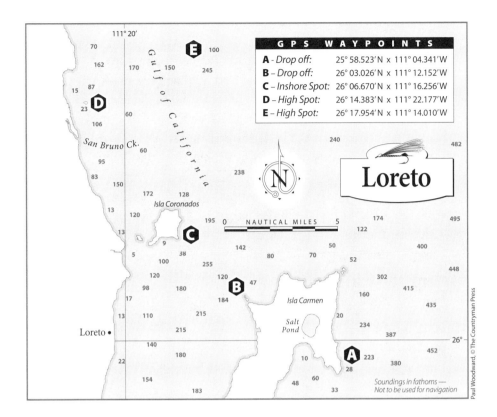

puts La Paz on the list of prime fishing destinations.

This is a place where, unless you are an expert angler with a detailed knowledge of the area and have your own boat, I recommend that you hire a guide to take you fishing offshore, at least on your first time out. With the help of a seasoned skipper, you will have a far better chance of racking up a prize catch.

But if you do decide to bring down your own private craft, also taking along a good depth finder and GPS unit will go a long way toward helping you to locate and mark any of the many drop-offs and rocky pinnacles in these waters that reliably produce fish.

Offshore, Isla Espirito Santo offers several spectacular, turquoise lagoons for those who like to snorkel or enjoy the sport of spearfishing. Just beyond, the deep blue waters on both sides of the island are prime territory for seasonal pelagic gamesters such as marlin, tuna, and dorado. Conversely, the adjoining, rock-strewn depths harbor huge, tackle-busting pargo that are patiently waiting to snatch your bait and have you then try desperately to pull them from their hiding places.

Map 13—Loreto Region

Loreto was once one of the most prolific areas in the entire Cortez for a multitude of fish species. Among the most prominent of these were the several species of giant grouper and sea bass that used to be easily located and caught by just about anybody who wanted one.

But, sadly, those days are long gone and, because of both extensive commercial and recreational fishing pressure, the region is now almost completely devoid of these beautiful fish, which used to regularly tip the scales at weights upwards of several hundred pounds. Even so, inshore anglers can still catch smaller pargo, cabrilla, and leopard grouper up to around 20 pounds, which for many these days is quite good enough.

Probably the most commonly targeted gamefish off of Loreto is now the yellowtail. One of the most productive areas is adjacent to Isla Del Carmen and, although trolling Rapalas, Yo-Zuris, and other popular hard baits may take most of the migrating yellowtail each season, the going can get a bit tough when the water begins to cool down during wintertime.

These are the months when anglers in the know bring out the bottom iron and start fishing for some of the big, homeguard yellowtail that stay around throughout the year, and are often caught on metal jigs near the bottom at depths of 120 feet or more.

Map 14—Punta Chivato/Mulegé Region

Punta Chivato is a popular fishing destination that pokes out into the Sea of Cortez less than 10 miles northeast of the palm-lined oasis of Mulegé. For many years, it was visited primarily by hardcore Baja anglers and RV groups, but since the construction of improved launching facilities and other infrastructure developments, it has become an extremely popular destination for private boaters who come to fish its still relatively prolific waters.

While there was a time when this area was known as a sure thing for those targeting large sea bass and grouper, several decades of intense commercial fishing pressure have reduced populations of these species to all-time lows. Nevertheless, anglers who ply the deep holes and pinnacles around the small, inshore islands known as Islas Santa Inés can still look forward to a host of snappers, cabrilla, and leopard grouper that are interested in taking their baits or lures.

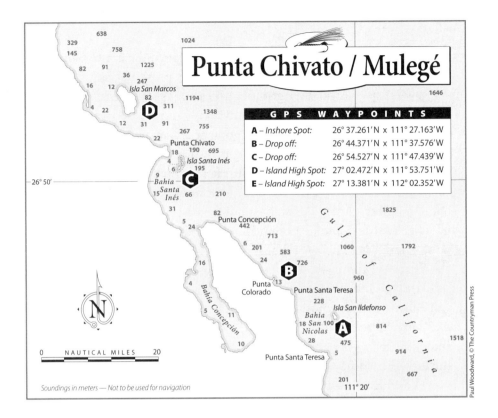

Punta Chivato / Mulegé

638
329
145
758
1024
82   91
1225
36
247
16   12   Isla San Marcos
82   1194
1646
4   22   D   311
1348
12   31   91   755
267
22   Punta Chivato
18   190   695
4   Isla Santa Inés
6   195

GPS WAYPOINTS

A – Inshore Spot: 26° 37.261'N x 111° 27.163'W
B – Drop off: 26° 44.371'N x 111° 37.576'W
C – Drop off: 26° 54.527'N x 111° 47.439'W
D – Island High Spot: 27° 02.472'N x 111° 53.751'W
E – Island High Spot: 27° 13.381'N x 112° 02.352'W

26° 50'
9
Bahia   C
15   Santa
Inés   66   210
31
82   1825
5   Punta Concepción
24   442
713
6   201   583
16   24   726
4   960
Punta   13
Colorado   Punta Santa Teresa
228   Isla San Ildefonso
Bahia
18   San 100   A
Nicolas   814
28   475
Punta Santa Teresa   5   914
667
201
111° 20'

Gulf of California

Bahía Concepción

N

0   NAUTICAL MILES   20

1060   1792

1518

Soundings in meters — Not to be used for navigation

Paul Woodward, © The Countryman Press

The offshore bite during summer can be absolutely sizzling in these waters. Yellowfin tuna, yellowtail, dorado, marlin, and even occasional sailfish are available several miles out. And, as with most pelagic species found in open water, almost all these fish are best located by keeping a keen eye on your sonar while simultaneously looking for working flocks of circling or diving birds.

Map 15—Bahía de Los Angeles

Bahía de Los Angeles, or L.A. Bay, as veteran Bajaphiles sometimes call it, is perhaps the most underdeveloped tourist "gold mine" on the entire east coast of Baja California. This magnificently pristine bay is studded with small desert islands that offer some of the most captivating views in the Sea of Cortez, yet it is practically barren by modern standards. One of the main reasons for this may be the 40-mile drive down the sometimes poorly maintained side road from the main highway that is required to reach the area.

Although commercial fishing pressure over the years has taken an

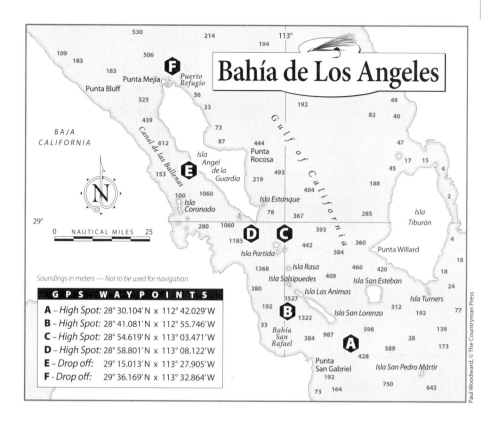

incredible toll on the once thriving population of various marine organisms propagating within the bay, there is still some great fishing to be had, as long as the wind doesn't come up. The farther offshore you venture, the more the seasonal northerly winds can become a problem.

To avoid potential disaster, when the north winds are blowing small craft should avoid fishing anywhere except in sheltered island coves that are very close to the main beach, and even that could be pushing the envelope a bit. When taking a boat out anywhere along the Baja coast, it is vitally important to keep a close eye on the weather, never venture any farther from shore than your boat can safely go, and *always* let common sense be your guide.

But, when the weather is calm, the sun is hot, and the water is glassy, Bahía de Los Angeles can be a fantastic place to wet a line. No matter whether you troll Rapalas around the islands for yellowtail, black skipjack, or barracuda, or drop your bait down into a rocky depression to hook a spotted bay bass or leopard grouper, L.A. Bay can still put a smile on the face of almost any angler.

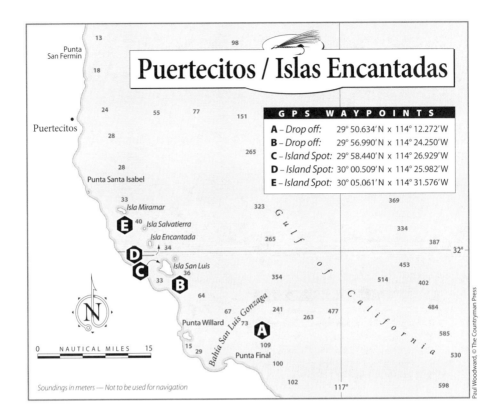

Map 16—Puertecitos/Islas Encantadas Region

About 50 miles south of San Felipe, Puertecitos features one of the only concrete launch ramps in the region. Even at that, it will never be mistaken for the marina at Cabo San Lucas. For being so close to the rapidly growing tourist town just to the north, this area along Baja's Cortez coast is truly rural in almost every sense of the word.

Don't expect to find a fancy hotel, a gourmet restaurant, or a vast array of amenities for the tourist here—the most beguiling land-based features around Puertecitos are the small volcanic hot springs that flow nearby. Out on the water, however, it is a different matter.

The Islas Encantadas, or Enchanted Islands, are just offshore a few miles down the coast and, because of the generally good fishing to be had there, are usually one of the stopping points for mothership panga operations that are based in San Felipe.

In addition to solid bottom fishing for leopard grouper, spotted bay bass, and cabrilla, the area around the islands is a prime place to catch large orangemouth corvina and white sea bass between June and September. The islands also feature great seasonal yellowtail fishing, and the many adjacent high spots offer perfect areas to throw and quickly retrieve iron jigs for a variety of species.

This entire section of coastline, between the south end at Punta Final and Puertecitos to the north, offers a wealth of open beaches and rocky coves to tempt the kayaker. In these waters, a digital fish finder can mean the difference between success and failure by assisting you to locate the structure on the bottom that draws and holds fish.

When targeting surface species during the summer months, slowly trolling a lure or rigged mackerel at about 5 knots a few hundred yards off the beach is likely to provoke a vicious strike from a roving white sea bass or yellowtail.

The Story
of the
Baja Panga

The Baja panga is a sturdy, dorylike boat built from wood and fiberglass, and has been used successfully for generations in small, rural fish camps located along Baja California's remote Pacific and Cortez coasts. Pangas usually measure about 22 feet in length, and feature a high bow and plenty of freeboard to handle the rough water in which they must often operate. Intrepid commercial fishermen have braved the ocean in these tough, seaworthy vessels for many years, and consistently manage to return to port with surprisingly large bounties for such relatively small craft.

Over time, many panga camps, particularly in Baja Norte, have developed the additional enterprise of creating sport fishing fleets to provide boats and guides for recreational anglers. Those who take the time to enjoy this more primitive method of inshore angling are usually rewarded with better fishing, bigger fish, and a greater degree of personalized service than is generally available on many of the larger commercial "cattle boats" that work out of Baja's major ports.

This often-overlooked style of sport fishing has been stocking the freezers of happy anglers for more than 40 years, and the time has come to alert those who have yet to try it of the great fun and opportunity that they have been missing. On the Pacific coast of Baja Norte, panga operations in places like Punta Banda, Puerto Santo Tomás, and Erindera have worked hard to build a longstanding reputation for being able to fill the burlap of their clients with a broad array of both inshore and deepwater species. The average price of a trip is quite reasonable, about $35 to $45 per person, based on three to five anglers per panga.

South of Ensenada, Capt. Cruz Zamora guides his clients to the fishing grounds through the surf. (LYNN GATCH)

Reservations are nearly always a must at the more popular camps, since you will usually need to arrange for a skipper and panga the day before your trip. You should also plan to bring your own gear and terminal tackle, since only a few of these camps have a reasonable selection of the hooks, weights, and lures that may be necessary when you are out on the water. Almost all the camps, however, feature modest overnight lodging—but you might want to bring along a flashlight and many of the personal items, beverages, bottled water, and snacks that you would normally take on a camping trip. Also, be sure to pack warm clothing, even if your trip is in the middle of summer. Intensely hot inland temperatures on the eastern side of the Baja peninsula will often pull in a thick, unseasonably cool marine layer along its Pacific coast, particularly during morning hours.

The drive toward Ensenada is punctuated by an increasing number of condominiums and other developments designed to cater to Americans seeking a weekend or retirement villa south of the border. Once past Ensenada, the main highway becomes a two-lane road. Beyond Maneadero, it is recommended that driving be done only during daylight hours.

Vonny's Fleet—Punta Banda

Of all the panga camps on Baja's Pacific coast, Ivan Villarino's Vonny's Fleet, just south of Ensenada, is perhaps one of the best equipped, as well as one of the closest operations to Southern California's vast angling population. The fleet's sturdy pangas launch from the beach at the calm, southern end of Bahía de Todos Santos, and fish the turquoise waters along Punta Banda's northern shore, and just off the rocky tip of the peninsula near La Bufadora. The Vonny's Fleet pangeros are excellent—lead Captain Beto Zamora is acclaimed as one of the most productive skippers in their area. Like many of the northern panga camps, Vonny's Fleet's primary focus is on lingcod and other rockfish. From spring through fall, however, it is also possible to catch a wide variety of popular gamefish like yellowtail, calico bass, halibut, sand bass, white sea bass, and large bonito. Web site: www.vonnysfleet.com/index.htm. Phone: 011-52-646-154-2046. E-mail: vonyflet@telnor.net.

Puerto Santo Tomás—Santo Tomás

Located south of Maneadero and Puente de las Animas, Puerto Santo Tomás offers some of the most remote and untapped sport fishing in Baja. Once they've negotiated the long, dusty drive along the graded road between the main highway and the coast, visitors to this primitive area can relax and enjoy some of the most profuse assemblages of local marine life that can be accessed on Baja's northern Pacific coast. Because of the relatively light angling pressure, many of the fish taken in this area are often larger specimens than are generally found in more populated regions.

Getting there can be a bit tricky, but follow these directions and you should be in great shape. Between kilometer markers 46 and 47, you will see a road sign on the right that reads PUERTO SANTO TOMÁS. Proceed approximately 150 feet past the road sign and make a right turn (west) onto a gravel road. (Note: If you reach the village of Santo Tomás on Highway #1, you've gone too far.) Continue on the gravel road for 18 miles. There will be forks in the road, but remember to *always* keep to the *right* and you'll be fine. At the end of the road, you will come to the coast. Veer to the right and climb the small hill, heading north. Go north along the coast for approximately 3 miles, and at the end of the road you will have finally arrived at Puerto Santo Tomás! Contact

Sam Saenz at www.puertosantotomas.com/bajadirections.htm. Phone: 011-52-646-1549415 E-mail: realbaja@starband.net.

Castro's Camp—Ejido Erendira

Castro's Camp is one of the longest-running panga operations on the Pacific coast, and is an ongoing favorite of numerous old-timers who began fishing the area over 40 years ago. This is the original Baja fish camp that inspired so many stories of small groups of gringo fishermen who would end up catching so many rock cod and other local species that they would each return home with several large coolers filled to the brim with the delicate, iced-down fillets. Fortunately, most of today's anglers tend to limit their "keepers" for the sake of the resource, but the fishing out of Castro's Camp is still exceptional, and even offers the opportunity to hook up with a big white sea bass between spring and fall.

The turnoff for Ejido Erendira is 180 km south of the border and at the 78 km marker south of Ensenada. Erendira is 12 miles down the asphalt road. Continue through the village toward the coast until you see Castro's sign on left. E-mail: castrosf@telnor.net. Phone: 011-52-646-176-2897. Fax: 011-52-617-72585.

Regardless of the location you ultimately select for your panga fishing trip, you are bound to encounter a truly different kind of angling experience, one which removes you from the hurried modern world, and briefly whisks you back to the days when those who fished were much closer to the elements that made their pastime worthwhile.

Panga Motherships

While pangas are usually available for hire on a daily basis in fishing destinations along both of Baja's coastlines, its eastern coast on the Sea of Cortez offers multiple-day panga sport fishing trips aboard large, well-equipped "motherships" that ply the waters between San Felipe and the Midriff Islands near Bahía de Los Angeles, and occasionally productive fishing areas even farther south.

Imagine yourself in a placid, turquoise cove. Although the sun has barely risen, you can already feel its intense rays warming your shoulders. The small panga carrying you and a few fellow anglers drifts slowly a couple of hundred yards from the lee side of a barren desert island only seconds before all hell breaks loose. Suddenly, your rod jolts and bends practically in half as the drag on your reel begins screaming.

The alert panga captain immediately throws the motor out of neutral and into reverse, backing the boat away from the rocks until you have a chance to regain control of the battle. After ten long minutes that seem more like an hour, your beautiful, 18-pound leopard grouper finally comes to gaff. After the euphoria has momentarily subsided, you happily realize that your first day on a multiday mothership panga trip has only just begun.

Ray Cannon, the father of Baja sport fishing, once referred to the Sea of Cortez as "the great fish trap" due to the fact that, for hundreds of miles, this narrow sea is tightly bordered by the coasts of Mexico and Baja California, and is open at only one end. As a result, these generally warm subtropical waters provide a nearly perfect sanctuary for the propagation of numerous species of fish and other marine life.

Over eons, volcanic upwellings have created numerous small islands and countless concealed grottos beneath the surface that harbor a vast array of hungry fish, many of which can weigh well over 100 pounds. Whether anglers are looking for huge, broomtail grouper and big cabrilla, or fat yellowtail, giant Humboldt squid, and white sea bass, a trip on a panga mothership provides a chance to experience the fishing adventure of a lifetime.

Well over a half century ago, San Felipe was a prime destination for dedicated anglers who were willing to make the dusty, daylong drive from Mexicali in pursuit of the legendary giant totuava.

In those days, totuava attained weights of several hundred pounds, and were one of the primary staples of San Felipe's economy. Years later, overharvesting and other management factors pushed this valuable fish to the brink of extinction. But anglers who visited the region during its prime had returned home with so many fantastic tales of big, hungry fish south of the border that the cat was already out of the bag.

Fortunately, after the collapse of the commercial totuava industry, a young fisherman in San Felipe named Gustavo Velez and his friend, Tony Reyes, came up with an idea that would end up changing the face of sport fishing along the entire northeast coast of Baja California. The concept of the panga mothership was born.

Until then, most sport fishing operations had made a business of crowding a couple of dozen fishermen together on a single boat, where lines tangled easily and tempers often frayed. Tony and Gustavo, however, dreamed of offering their clients a large, livable craft that would

Pangas in tow behind the Cortez mothership *Erik*.   (DANA KERBY)

tow a small armada of pangas down the rugged Baja coast to fish the
abundantly rich waters that surround the many rocky islands in the
upper Gulf.

Anglers would then be able to fish selected coves from a small craft
with no more than two or three passengers per boat, and then enjoy
the luxury of returning to a hot shower, a warm meal, and a good
nights sleep before doing it all again the next day.

After acquiring a veteran shrimp trawler, *General Felipe Angeles*,
and making the necessary adaptations, such as providing sleeping accommodations, an upgraded galley, restrooms, and a terrace, Velez and
Reyes were in business. Once anglers from north of the border got a
taste of this kind of action, and brought back coolers full of succulent
grouper, cabrilla, and pargo fillets, their passenger rosters began to fill
rapidly. Some time later, years of prosperity allowed Gustavo and Tony
to part on friendly terms and pursue their own separate goals.

In 1980, Gustavo Velez began building what was to be Mexico's
largest sport fishing craft, the 125-foot *Andrea Lynn*, which he named
after his daughter. Unfortunately, a complicated turn of economic and
political events eventually caused the project to lay stagnant for well
over a decade. But after the construction of the *Andrea Lynn* was put

on hold, the changed circumstances provided Gustavo with the opportunity to visit Europe and purchase a sturdy, steel-hulled Dutch Navy survey boat, the *Norvander,* which he then transported to San Felipe and began operating under the banner of Baja Sportfishing, Inc.

Today, Gustavo's 105-foot steel vessel, renamed *Erik,* is fully air conditioned and equipped with a gourmet galley, comfortable staterooms, and upper deck to provide the next level of comfort and relaxation for passengers during either hot summer weather or occasionally rough seas. The story of the *Andrea Lynn,* however, remains full of twists and turns.

In 1995, Gustavo finally ended up selling the *Andrea Lynn* to a Mexican investment group, who provided more than $2 million in funding to complete work on the boat. After its launch in the early summer of 2000, she remained anchored in San Felipe for more than a year until being moved over to Puerto Vallarta on the Mexican mainland, and finally being transported up the coast to Puerto Peñasco, where a fire destroyed the craft's upper structure. Luckily, there was no damage to the hull, engines, and below-decks refrigeration units.

After Gustavo learned what had happened, he quickly reacquired the *Andrea Lynn* and returned it once again to San Felipe, where it was completely refurbished and put back into service in the summer of 2006. Today, it is professionally staffed by a uniformed crew, and features 10 large staterooms on the main deck level that can accommodate

The 105-foot, steel-hulled *Erik* at anchor (DANA KERBY)

up to three passengers each, with every stateroom enjoying the luxury of its own bathroom and shower. There is also a well-stocked cocktail bar and a large galley adjacent to the dining room on the top level.

Although the *Andrea Lynn* operates primarily as a classic, state-of-the-art panga mothership, it can also accommodate scuba diving and snorkeling charters, and has been fitted with facilities to transport kayaks as well. She regularly tows ten sturdy, 23-foot pangas, each complete with live bait wells and equipped with well-maintained, 75-horsepower outboard motors and GPS fish finders. Most important, in the interest of passenger safety each of the guides is in possession of a VHF radio with which he can stay in constant communication with the mothership.

In addition to Gustavo's Baja Sportfishing, Inc. and Tony Reyes Sportfishing, there is also Sea of Cortez Sportfishing, owned by Bobby Castellon. Motherships from all three companies sail from San Felipe. Trips generally run between five and six days in length, include all meals, and are reasonably priced at well under $1,000 per angler, which is an exceptional bargain in today's world.

For more than a decade, Gustavo's operation has thrived under the marketing guidance of Dana and Jim Kerby, who regularly make sure that all their clients' needs are accommodated. During the off season, you will find these two avid Baja enthusiasts in attendance at trade shows around the United States, armed with plenty of photographic evidence to prove that fishing from a small panga near the rugged islands in the upper Sea of Cortez is a one-of-a-kind experience.

But no matter which operation you choose to fish with, the serene and enchanting environment in the upper Sea of Cortez will mesmerize you, especially after spending a few blissful days out on the water. Whether you're using artificial lures or live bait, it will quickly become apparent why the islands of the upper Cortez are considered to have some of the best saltwater fishing in the entire Northern Hemisphere.

A Taste of Baja

La cocina Mexicana, the Mexican kitchen, lies at the very heart of Baja culture. The family reigns supreme throughout Mexico, and it is the kitchen that fuels the family.

Although larger cities like Tijuana, Ensenada, La Paz, and Cabo San Lucas offer the typically modern grocery stores that most Americans have become accustomed to, a majority of the people living throughout Baja rely on the small farmers' markets, fish stands, and produce carts available in almost every poblado to supply their daily household needs.

Because Baja California is almost entirely surrounded by salt water, most residents also depend heavily upon edible treasures from the sea to supplement their diets. Here are some recipes that will assist you in delighting yourself and your guests with delicious south-of-the-border cuisine.

¡El Choro De Viva! (Pursuing the Marvelous Mussel)

Baja slang can sometimes be a bit confusing for new visitors, particularly when the words sound similar. Let's see now—"churros"? No, those are the long, deep-fried, sugar-covered pastry sticks that the vendors keep trying to sell you near La Bufadora, just south of Ensenada. Hm. "Charros"? Nope! That's just another name for a vaquero, or a cowboy. All right, then, let's try "choros," those tasty little black mussels. Ah, yes, now *that's* what I'm talking about!

While you may read my suggestions for using mussels as one of the most effective baits for catching a variety of inshore gamefish along most of Baja's Pacific coast, it is important to note that, during the winter months, they are also viewed as prized table fare and pursued by a number of ungainly, bipedal land dwellers as well. Most of Baja Norte's seafood lovers agree that there's nothing quite like a big plate of succulent choros de ajo or a steaming bowl of caldo de choro on a chilly evening.

Mytilus californianus are the largest species of mussel on the West Coast of North America, and range from Baja California to the Gulf of Alaska. These bivalve mollusks often form thick beds on exposed sections of rocky shoreline adjacent to the surf zone and spawn throughout the year, with peak activity occurring during spring and fall.

Baja Norte's mussels are considered prime epicurean table fare during the winter months. Coastal Native Americans have known this for thousands of years, and modern residents still enjoy feasting on them today. They pair wonderfully with linguine and pesto sauce, are absolutely mandatory when making Spanish paella, and are exquisite when simply steamed and dipped in garlic butter.

During the summer, however, you should avoid eating these mussels, because they may become extremely poisonous when concentrations of toxins from the noxious plankton *Gonyaula* build up in their flesh. In Southern California waters, mussels are generally quarantined between May 1 and October 31 and should not be eaten during those months in northern Baja, either.

For those with a desire to head down to the beach and try harvesting a fresh dinner from the sea, I have a few suggestions. First of all, it's winter—dress warmly! You will also need a sturdy pair of garden gloves, a bucket or a burlap sack, and a stout pry bar, such as a tire iron or a large screwdriver, to get the choros off of the rocks. As a safety precaution, I strongly advise against going hunting for choros alone. Each year, thousands of people around the world are swept off coastal rocks to their deaths after being hit by a rogue wave when they least expected it.

Always go when the tidal cycle is at its lowest point, and collect the smallest mussels you can find that are still of an edible size. While big choros offer more meat for chowders, the small ones are the very sweetest for enjoying on the half shell.

After you have returned home and have scrubbed and debearded your catch, here is a recipe that is bound to make you a celebrity with everyone at your dinner table.

Choros Baja

> 2 kilos small black choros (mussels),
>   scrubbed and debearded in the shell
> $2\frac{1}{2}$ to 3 cups of fish stock
> 2 tablespoons olive oil
> 2 yellow onions cut into julienne strips
> $\frac{1}{2}$ teaspoon salt
> $\frac{1}{2}$ teaspoon freshly ground black pepper
> 4 cloves garlic, well minced
> 1 cup tomato juice
> $1\frac{1}{2}$ cups dry white wine
> 1 tablespoon dried, freshly crushed oregano
> 1 teaspoon saffron threads
> $\frac{1}{2}$ cup fresh cilantro, coarsely chopped

In a large, heavy-bottomed saucepan over medium heat, add 1 tablespoon of the olive oil, half the onions, salt, and pepper, and then sauté, stirring briskly until the onions are translucent. Add the garlic and sauté for one minute longer. Then add the white wine and bring to a boil. Boil until reduced by half, seven or eight minutes. Add the oregano, saffron, fish stock, and tomato juice and bring to a boil. Reduce the heat to low and simmer for 10 minutes to blend the flavors. Strain through a sieve into a bowl and set aside.

Place two large, wide sauté pans over high heat. Add half the remaining tablespoon of olive oil to each pan. Add half the remaining onions to each pan and sauté briefly, stirring occasionally, until they just begin to color, about four minutes. Add half the mussels to each pan, spreading them out in a single layer. Sauté and stir occasionally for a few minutes. Add half the strained broth to each pan and bring to a boil.

Reduce heat to medium, cover, and simmer until all the mussels have opened. Discard any that do not open.

Add half the chopped cilantro to each pan. Toss to mix, and then spoon the mussels into warmed shallow soup bowls. Divide the broth evenly among the bowls and serve immediately with warm bolillos.

Shrimp

The Baja Peninsula has been blessed with numerous gifts from the sea, and each year the people living near the productive waters in the upper Sea of Cortez celebrate that fact with late fall shrimp festivals to express their great love for these succulent crustaceans.

Here's a recipe that includes the rich, earthy flavor of poblano chilis to help spice things up a bit. One important tip is to always select the best ingredients. When buying fresh shrimp, be sure to insist on purchasing only ones that are firm, and lacking in even the slightest hint of ammonia. In the event that a suitably fresh product is unavailable, try to find frozen shrimp that have been individually quick-frozen.

The poblano chili pepper ranges in color from dark green to almost black and have a tempting, rich flavor that can vary from mild to picante. The darkest poblanos generally have the most intense flavor, making them the best candidates for stuffing. Although poblano chilis are grown throughout the southwestern United States and are readily available in most supermarkets, many epicureans say that the very best-tasting chilis are still found in central Mexico.

Fresh shrimp is a household staple around coastal Baja, and it is usually available in a variety of sizes. (LYNN GATCH)

Poblano-Shrimp Enchiladas

$\frac{1}{2}$ kilo fresh, unpeeled medium shrimp
8 tablespoons olive oil, divided
1 large poblano chili, halved and seeded
1 large onion, finely chopped
2 cloves garlic, peeled and finely chopped
1 tomato, coarsely chopped
$\frac{1}{2}$ teaspoon salt
1 teaspoon dried Mexican oregano
$\frac{1}{4}$ teaspoon freshly ground cumin seed
$\frac{1}{4}$ teaspoon black pepper
$\frac{1}{2}$ cup sour cream
8 to 10 freshly made corn tortillas
1 10- or 12-ounce can of tomatillo- and
    green chili-based enchilada sauce
$1\frac{1}{2}$ cups (6–8 ounces) shredded Manchego
    or Monterey Jack cheese

Peel, devein, and rinse the shrimp, then set aside. Brush an 11 x 7 inch baking dish with 2 tablespoons of olive oil, and set aside. Sauté pepper in remaining oil in a large skillet over medium-high heat until skin looks blistered. Remove from skillet, and chop.

While canned tomatillo salsa works well in most Baja recipes, and is practically a proverb in most regional kitchens, there is nothing quite like the fresh product for adorning seafood, chicken, and pork dishes. This simple recipe makes creating cocina gastrónomo easy.

Fresh Tomatillo Salsa

14 fresh tomatillos
6 cloves of garlic, peeled
3 chilis Serranos
1 bunch fresh cilantro, top leaves only
$\frac{1}{4}$ teaspoon cumin seeds, crushed
$\frac{1}{2}$ teaspoon freshly ground black pepper
$\frac{1}{2}$ teaspoon salt

Remove all the husks from the tomatillos, and then rinse them in warm water to help remove any additional debris. In a shallow baking dish, broil all the ingredients except the cilantro in a preheated 450-

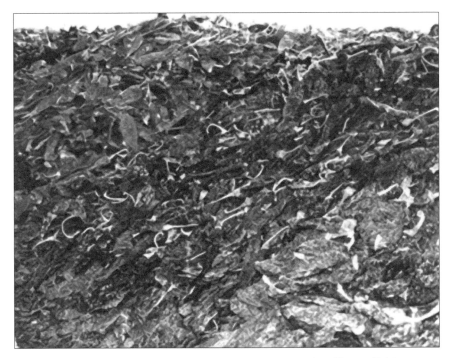

Farmers' markets in Mexico offer the widest variety of chilis available almost anywhere in the world. (LYNN GATCH)

degree oven until they begin to brown. Turn off the broiler and allow the dish to remain in the oven a few more minutes. Place mixture and fresh cilantro into a food processor, and then blend until smooth. Use as either a cooking sauce or as table salsa.

Sopa Siete Mares (Baja's Seven Seas Soup)

The quintessential soup of the Baja peninsula, sopa siete mares has almost as many versions as there are poblados in both Baja Norte and Sur. Feel free to adjust these ingredients and seasonings to suit your own personal taste—everyone else does!

Base:
4 unpeeled garlic cloves
8 medium-large dried guajillo chilis,
    seeded and stemmed
$\frac{1}{2}$ Tbsp. dried whole Mexican oregano
$\frac{1}{4}$ teaspoon freshly ground black pepper
Large pinch of freshly ground cumin seeds

2 tablespoons Extra Virgin olive oil
$\frac{1}{2}$ cup water

Over medium heat, roast the garlic in a heavy skillet, constantly turning until it is soft and lightly browned. Let the cloves cool, and then peel. Toast the chilis one or two at a time using the same skillet, flattening them for a few seconds on each side with a spatula. Cover the toasted chilis with boiling water and steep for about 30 minutes, stirring occasionally. Drain the chilis thoroughly and add them together in a food processor along with the crushed cumin seeds, black pepper, roasted garlic, and $\frac{1}{2}$ cup of water. Blend the mixture into a smooth purée, adding more water if necessary. Strain through a medium mesh colander. Heat the olive oil in a large soup pot and add the purée once it has begun to sizzle. Set aside.

Soup:
4 quarts fish or shellfish broth
1 large bunch of fresh cilantro
2 teaspoons salt
1 tablespoon brown or raw sugar
14 large (or 18 medium) shrimp, heads on
5 small potatoes, boiled and diced
2 cups diced chayote squash
    (zucchini can be substituted)
4 medium onions, finely minced
1 kilo of fresh, well-scrubbed clams, mussels,
    or a combination of both
1 kilo of boneless, skinless white fish fillet
    such as rock cod, sea bass, or halibut, cut into cubes

Combine ingredients and bring to a boil, then reduce heat and simmer for 15 minutes before adding the strained base mixture. Continue to cook over medium heat for 45 minutes while stirring occasionally. Peel and devein the shrimp, leaving the tails on. Add the potatoes to the hot broth. Simmer uncovered until the potatoes are nearly tender, about five minutes. Add the zucchini and cook for three minutes. Add the mussels or clams and simmer until the shellfish open, then add the fish cubes before stirring in the shrimp. Cover, remove from heat, and let stand for at least five minutes before serving.

Garnish with chopped white onions, minced cilantro, and lime wedges. Enjoy with fresh, warm tortillas.

Abalone

Over the past half century, the highly prized abalone has virtually disappeared from the coast of Southern California. The Pacific coast of Baja Norte is now one of the few places where you can still find what is arguably one of the most coveted gastropods on our planet. Please be advised, however, that it is illegal for visitors in Mexico to harvest them. Some commercial fishermen, local fish markets, and divers will occasionally sell them, but it is a good idea to know whom you are dealing with so as not to run afoul of the law. You may substitute calamari steak in this recipe if you can't find any reasonably priced abalone, but avoid buying anything being offered as "abulón" if it is bright orange in color; this is a characteristic of large limpets that may look a bit like abalone, but are as tough as shoe leather.

Should you be lucky enough to end up with a few of these elegantly flavored, albeit pricey, univalve mollusks, the following recipe will provide a great alternative preparation to simply breading and sautéing the tenderized medallions.

Baja is rich in local seafood of all kinds. Here, the owner of a Punta Banda seafood market near Ensenada shows off his catch of the day—giant spider crabs that are caught at depths greater than 1,000 feet. (LYNN GATCH)

Abalone Chowder

1 quart water
1 teaspoon salt
4 large red potatoes
1 pound raw tenderized abalone, cut into
    $\frac{1}{4}$-inch cubes (substitute calamari if desired)
6 slices bacon, chopped
$\frac{1}{4}$ cup sliced jalapeño peppers (canned)
1 medium white onion, chopped
$\frac{1}{4}$ cup all-purpose flour
$\frac{1}{2}$ teaspoon salt
$\frac{1}{8}$ teaspoon pepper
$\frac{1}{8}$ teaspoon dried thyme leaves
3 cups milk
1 small bay leaf
$1\frac{1}{2}$ cups light whipping cream
2 tablespoons sesame oil

In a preheated skillet, heat the sesame oil and quickly fry the abalone cubes until golden brown. Set aside.

Boil the water in a 2-quart saucepan, and then add the potatoes and salt. Return the water to a boil, then reduce heat and simmer the potatoes for half an hour. Drain and cool the potatoes, then peel and cut into small cubes. Set aside.

Over medium to high heat, cook the bacon in a Dutch oven until crisp, stirring occasionally. Remove and set aside. Add the onion and jalapeños and then cook a few minutes, stirring until tender.

Reduce heat and stir in the milk, flour, pepper, salt, and thyme. Continue to stir constantly until the mixture is bubbly and has thickened. Reduce heat to low, blend in the cream, and then add the potato cubes and abalone. While gently stirring, simmer over low heat for another 10 to 12 minutes. Garnish liberally with sliced scallions and serve with warm bolillo rolls.

Fish Tacos

Visitors to the coastal regions of Baja have turned the fish taco into what is now one of the most fashionable fast foods throughout the United States. One of the most prominent versions of this specialty is served in San Felipe, the famed fishing and shrimping port at the northern end of the Sea of Cortez.

Fish Tacos—San Felipe Style

    1 to 2 pounds of sea bass, halibut,
        or rock cod fillet, cut into
        2- to 3-inch-long strips
    1 fresh head of green cabbage,
        very finely shredded
    2 limes cut into wedges
    12 freshly made corn tortillas
    $\frac{1}{2}$ to 1 cup corn or vegetable oil

Heat oil in a skillet until it is very hot. Rinse fillet strips well, and then pat with paper towels until perfectly dry. Dip fish into batter and place in skillet so that the pieces are not touching each other. Cook the fish on all sides until it is just golden brown and lightly crisp. Remove pieces from pan and drain well. Remove remaining oil from the skillet and gently heat the tortillas until they are soft. Place a few fish pieces onto each warm tortilla, and then top with shredded cabbage, salsa blanca, tomato salsa, and a lime wedge. Serve immediately. This recipe also works well with shrimp and lobster.

The local fish market in Ensenada, referred to as the Mercado Negro ("black market"), carries seafood and fish of nearly every type imaginable.
(LYNN GATCH)

South-of-the-Border Beer Batter

> 1 cup white flour
> 3 cloves of garlic, very finely minced
> $\frac{1}{2}$ teaspoon freshly ground black pepper
> $\frac{1}{4}$ cup canned jalapeño slices,
>   well chopped
> 8 ounces Mexican beer

Mix all ingredients together well and let stand at least a half hour before battering fish strips.

San Felipe-Style Salsa Blanca

> $\frac{1}{2}$ cup mayonnaise
> $\frac{1}{2}$ cup plain yogurt
> $\frac{1}{2}$ fresh lime, juiced

Whip ingredients together vigorously, and then let chill in refrigerator or ice chest for 30 minutes to one hour before serving.

A common sight in coastal Baja is the local mariscos, or seafood stand. This one in San Felipe has the bragging rights of being located in the town that gave birth to the fish taco popular in the United States today.
(LYNN GATCH)

Salsa de Chili Arbol

This salsa is best when made using tomatoes that have fully ripened naturally. If they are not available, canned tomatoes may be substituted.

4 pods of dried chilis arbol, crushed
6 fresh, ripe tomatoes or substitute
    2 cups canned tomatoes
One 8-ounce can of tomato sauce
1 medium white onion, well chopped
1 fresh lime, juiced
4 cloves of finely minced fresh garlic
$\frac{1}{2}$ teaspoon freshly crushed cumin seeds
1 teaspoon whole dried Mexican oregano,
    freshly crushed
$\frac{1}{2}$ teaspoon salt
$\frac{1}{2}$ teaspoon fresh ground black pepper

Place the crushed chilis in a mixing bowl. Cover the chilis with 1 cup of very hot water and let steep for a couple of minutes. In a saucepan over medium heat, combine the remaining ingredients with the chili and chili water and simmer for a couple of minutes. If the salsa is too thick, thin with water to desired consistency. Pour the salsa into a bowl and allow it to sit at room temperature for an hour to help blend the flavors before serving. For a smoother end product, put the salsa into a blender or food processor and purée until it reaches the desired consistency.

Snapper

While the true red snapper, known throughout Baja as *huachinango*, is caught predominantly off of the western coast of Baja Sur and in much of the Sea of Cortez, certain rockfishes along the Pacific coast of Baja Norte are also sometimes referred to as "red snapper." Although unrelated, both these species are white-fleshed, delicately flavored, and absolutely superb when properly prepared. This special recipe includes a flavorful, long green chili as a delicious wrap for each of the delicate fillets.

Huachinango en Salsa Verde con Chilis Verdes

8 fillets of fresh red snapper, pargo, or rock cod

1 bunch fresh cilantro, well rinsed and patted dry

1 white onion, coarsely chopped

6 cloves fresh garlic, finely minced

6 peeled, de-ribbed and seeded fresh Anaheim
 or Hatch green chilis

2 fresh jalapeño chilis, seeded with
 stems removed

1 can of whole tomatillos, well rinsed

$\frac{1}{2}$ cup clarified butter

1 teaspoon freshly ground black pepper

1 teaspoon salt

4 cups of precooked saffron or Mexican-style rice,
 served hot

Place onion, garlic, cilantro, tomatillos, and jalapeños in a food processor and blend ingredients until they are completely blended. Cut each Anaheim (California) or Hatch (New Mexico) green chili lengthwise, remove all seeds and membranes, and then flatten them out with the inner side facing up, and set aside. Preheat your oven to 375 degrees. Melt butter in a skillet over medium heat. Combine the flour, black pepper, and salt in a shallow bowl. Dip the fillets in the flour mixture and sauté them gently in clarified butter, turning once, until each is lightly golden brown. Wrap each fish fillet in a green chili, arrange wrapped fillets on an ovenproof platter, and top with salsa verde. Place in oven until the salsa and chilis are well heated, and serve with warm tortillas and rice.

Smoke It!

Let's face it: you can only keep so many bags of fish steaks and fillets in your freezer. Some like to can their fish, so that they are able to enjoy tasty sandwiches and salads well into the next season. The only problem is you have to be very cautious to avoid the risk of contamination during the process. As a result, canning is probably best left to those who really know what they are doing. The next best way of preserving your catch is by having it smoked. This service is available at most major sport fishing landings, but there's often a lot more fun and satisfaction involved in doing the job yourself.

Although tuna and yellowtail are the prime candidates for the smoker, several of our more common local surface species, such as fresh bonito or barracuda, can also be easily transformed into gourmet fare. You can build your own smoker, or choose from one of the many brands that are commercially available. One of my favorites happens to be the Little Chief, available at a number of sporting goods outlets.

Actually, the basic formula for smoking fish is quite simple. Along with your favorite beverage, some fresh salsa, and a stack of saltines, this is a recipe that is practically guaranteed to keep your home full of cheerful visitors over the next couple of months.

Basic Smoking Brine

In a crock or glass container, thoroughly mix:

1 gallon water
1 cup Riesling or Chablis
1 cup salt
1 cup brown sugar
2 Serrano chilis, finely diced
2 tablespoons dry mustard
2 tablespoons black peppercorns, whole
2 lemons, quartered
6 bay leaves
8 cloves garlic, coarsely chopped

Use two whole tuna or yellowtail, 15 to 25 pounds each, which have been filleted into quarters with *all* the dark meat removed. Cut each quarter in half, and place it in the brine. Cover, refrigerate, and allow mixture to marinate for six to eight hours. Remove the fish from the brine, rinse in cold water, and let dry briefly on smoking racks.

Quickly sear the fish over charcoal until striped, and then place it in the smoker. If you have a drip pan, place 2 cups of white wine and 1 cup of Italian dressing in the pan. Slowly smoke the fish over low-temperature, smoldering mesquite or oak chips for three to four hours. Wrap well, and be sure to refrigerate or freeze all the smoked fish that will not be eaten immediately. If properly wrapped, it can remain frozen for several months.

Botanas y Bebidas (Appetizers and Drinks)

Cocktail time in Baja California is generally viewed as a very serious thing among its aficionados, particularly in remote coastal regions where it usually arrives at the conclusion of an adventurous and productive day on the water. Enjoying snacks and drinks at the end of the workday with family, friends, and lively conversation is an integral part of the Baja lifestyle. Here are a couple of suggestions to help get things started.

Ceviche

Ceviche is one of the most popular appetizers in all of Baja. Almost every coastal region has its own rendition of this mixture of raw shrimp, fish, or scallops, which naturally "cooks" itself in fresh citrus juice. Although there are many recipes to choose from, here are a couple of my personal favorites.

Scallop Ceviche

During the winter months, there always seem to be an abundance of those tasty little bay scallops in Baja fish markets. While they are a bit too small to cook individually, bay scallops are generally used in tacos, burritos, and perhaps most deliciously in ceviche. Here's a simple recipe that is bound to get your guests smacking their lips!

> 1 pound bay scallops (fresh or freshly defrosted)
> 4 fresh limes
> 1 fresh lemon
> $\frac{1}{2}$ medium red bell pepper, finely diced
> 1 medium red onion, finely diced
> 2 Serrano (hot) or 3 jalapeño (milder) chilis,
>   seeded and minced
> 2 cloves garlic, finely minced
> $\frac{1}{4}$ cup chopped, fresh cilantro
> 3 tablespoons extra-virgin olive oil
> 1 big pinch of whole, dried oregano, freshly crushed
> Salt to taste

Cut zest from one of the limes and the lemon in long strips. Squeeze $\frac{1}{2}$ cup lime juice and $\frac{1}{4}$ cup lemon juice. Combine citrus juice and zest, scallops, peppers, onion, chili, garlic, coriander, oregano, and oil in a mixing bowl. Marinate at room temperature, stirring occasionally, for one hour. Refrigerate covered for one hour. Remove zest from ceviche and season to taste with salt, if needed. Garnish with julienned lime zest.

Ceviche La Fiesta

This recipe is a specialty of Executive Chef Raul Delgadillo at La Fiesta, a popular restaurant in San Diego's Gaslamp Quarter, and is typical of the version served in Acapulco. It pairs wonderfully with crunchy corn tortilla chips, guacamole, and a cold cerveza or margarita.

$1\frac{1}{2}$ pounds white sea bass or other mild, white fish
2 pounds shrimp (31/40 size)
1 cup fresh lemon juice
1 cup fresh lime juice
1 cup fresh orange juice
$\frac{1}{3}$ cup olive oil
4 cloves fresh garlic
2 pounds ripe tomatoes
1 cup Spanish red onion
$\frac{1}{3}$ cup fresh cilantro tops, chopped
$\frac{1}{2}$ cup tomato catsup
1 tablespoon fresh oregano
$\frac{1}{2}$ teaspoon salt
$\frac{1}{4}$ teaspoon freshly ground black pepper
2 tablespoons Serrano chilis, finely chopped
$\frac{2}{3}$ cup green olives, coarsely chopped
1 ripe Hass avocado, sliced

Place the seafood in a glass bowl, cover with the citrus juice mixture, and refrigerate overnight.

Heat the olive oil in a small skillet; add the garlic and sauté for about three minutes. Discard the garlic and allow the oil to cool.

Chop tomatoes and remove seeds, but reserve the juice. Place in a large glass bowl and add the onion, cilantro, catsup, oregano, salt, pepper, chilis, and olives. Then add the skillet oil and mix well. Set aside.

Thoroughly rinse the seafood, cover again with fresh water, and let stand for five minutes, then rinse again. Add the seafood to the mixture of condiments and stir well. Serve immediately with avocado garnish, and enjoy!

Jalapeños Rellenos de Pescado Ahumado (Jalapeños Stuffed with Smoked Fish)

Smoked fish, usually either tuna or marlin, is extremely common in Baja markets during the summer months. Here's a popular home-style recipe that is very tasty, and is especially popular among those with a bountiful supply of these particular gamefish, and who ultimately end up soaking and smoking a portion of their catch.

> 20 medium-size jalapeño peppers, cut once
>   lengthwise with all seeds and
>   membranes removed
> 1 pound smoked tuna or marlin, flaked
> $\frac{1}{2}$ cup of shredded Manchego, Chihuahua,
>   or Monterey Jack cheese
> $\frac{1}{4}$ cup extra-virgin olive oil
> 2 cloves of fresh garlic, peeled and finely minced
> $\frac{1}{4}$ cup red onion, well diced
> 3 to 4 slices of smoked bacon, cut into
>   1- to 1$\frac{1}{2}$-inch pieces and cooked crisp
> $\frac{1}{4}$ tsp. sea salt
> $\frac{1}{2}$ tsp. freshly ground black pepper

In a small skillet, sauté the bacon pieces until crisp. Drain the cooked bacon on paper towels and set aside. Sauté garlic, onion, salt, and pepper in the olive oil until lightly translucent. Add the smoked fish and continue cooking for a few more minutes before removing the pan from the heat and quickly mixing in the shredded cheese until the filling is thoroughly blended. Stuff a piece of bacon and some of the mixture into each of the jalapeños, and place them on a lightly oiled grill over glowing coals. Allow the peppers to roast well, while occasionally turning each pepper until all sides are evenly cooked. Remove from grill and allow to cool for a few minutes before serving. As you might suspect, this recipe goes exceptionally well with a glass of cold Mexican beer.

Agua Fresca

The "aguas frescas" that are familiar to most Americans are those offered in some of the more authentic Mexican-style restaurants: horchata, jamiaca, and tamarindo. These types of non-alcoholic beverages are mealtime favorites, and are popular among young and old alike. This recipe is enjoyed primarily in Baja Norte, which produces an annual bounty of fresh cantaloupe for the world market. But it is equally flavorful and refreshing when watermelon, mango, or papaya is substituted as the featured fruit.

Agua de Melón (Cantaloupe Water)

>   1 cantaloupe, diced, seeds and rind removed
>   1 lime, juiced
>   6 cups of filtered or purified water
> $\frac{1}{2}$ cup sugar

Place half the cantaloupe into a blender, along with the lime juice and 2 cups of the water. Blend at high speed until liquefied, pour into a pitcher, and put aside. Place the rest of the melon in the blender with 2 cups of water; blend thoroughly and pour into the pitcher. Add the remaining 2 cups of water and the sugar into the pitcher and stir vigorously until the sugar is completely dissolved. Chill well before serving over a few ice cubes.

The Margarita

Although the margarita is perhaps the most famed cocktail ever attributed to the Republic of Mexico, few realize that its creation is actually credited to a man who lived in Tijuana, only a few miles across the border from San Diego, California.

Carlos Herrera, who passed away in 1992, is said to have invented the drink at Rancho La Gloria, a restaurant that he opened at his home just south of Tijuana in 1935. He told friends that it was sometime between 1938 and 1939 that he decided to mix a jigger of tequila with lemon juice, shaved ice, and triple sec and serve it in a salt-rimmed glass.

As the legend goes, one of his customers was a showgirl and occasional actress known as Marjorie King. Because she was supposedly allergic to all hard liquor except tequila, which she refused to drink straight, Herrera is said to have experimented with several combinations, and eventually named the best one "margarita" after her.

Since those days, the margarita has undergone many changes and has been mixed with strawberries, peaches, and just about everything else in the kitchen that you can think of. Some have even changed the recipe in regard to the types of liqueurs used to blend with the tequila. Today, it is most likely that a margarita in Baja Norte will contain the more potent Mexican orange liqueur, Controy, in lieu of the original triple sec. In Baja Sur, a margarita might also include Damiana Liqueur, which is made from the wild regional herb of the same name.

North of the border, exclusive cocktail lounges often offer margaritas made with either Grand Marnier or Courvoisier for their discriminating clientele. But any way you slice it, and no matter how you choose to make it, the margarita has become one of the most commonly served cocktails on the entire planet.

The following margarita recipe was created at the famous Hussong's Cantina in Ensenada, Baja Norte, and is guaranteed to liven up practically any occasion.

Hussong's Margarita (On the Rocks)

> 2 ounces Cuervo Gold Tequila
> $\frac{7}{8}$ ounce Mexican Controy
> 1 ounce freshly squeezed lime juice

Salt a cold champagne glass by wiping a cut lime around the rim and dipping into coarse salt to a depth of $\frac{1}{8}$ inch. Put the ingredients into a shaker with an abundance of cold, fresh ice. Cap the shaker and shake the margarita well. Strain into the prepared glass.

Do You Like Piña Coladas?

The earliest known reference to the piña colada in print was in the December 1922 issue of *Travel* magazine, which offered, " . . . but best of all is a piña colada; the juice of a perfectly ripe pineapple, a delicious drink in itself, rapidly shaken up with ice, sugar, lime and rum in delicate proportions. What could be more luscious, mellow and fragrant?"

Since then, the cocktail's recipe has continued to be refined and further celebrated in legend and song. And, with its ready access to fresh pineapples, coconuts, and rum it seems natural that the Baja peninsula is one of the very best places to enjoy one. The basic recipe that follows may be adjusted to suit your taste and tolerance.

2 cups ice cubes
¾ cup fresh pineapple, frozen
2 ounces fresh pineapple juice
2 ounces thick, canned coconut cream
    (Coco Lopez is one of the best)
1½ ounces amber rum
1½ ounces of black or dark rum
2 fresh pineapple wedges

In an electric blender, combine ice, rums, coconut cream, pineapple juice, and chunks. Blend on high speed until the mixture is icy smooth and frothy. Pour into two tall cocktail glasses that have been garnished with pineapple slices, and enjoy on a warm afternoon.

Baja Personalities

Scott Kennedy

Scott Kennedy grew up in Newport Beach during the late 1960s but never quite fit in with the rest of his peers. While they focused diligently on competitive sports and their teachers' classroom dissertations, young Scott always preferred staring out the window and watching the clouds drift by.

He also had a love for sketching and, early on, demonstrated an ability to render artistic impressions of the people and things around him with uncanny accuracy. Today we are all the richer, because the works of famed maritime artist Scott O. Kennedy now hang on the walls of art connoisseurs and dignitaries around the globe.

The legendary J. Russell Jinishian, long recognized as the nation's leading authority on contemporary marine art, once expressed the opinion: "Nobody can sit down quite the way Scott Kennedy does, with a simple pen and piece of paper, and make sense out of all that they are looking at in such a beautiful and elegant way."

Perhaps that is one of the reasons why his work was selected by Fox Studios to be used in their popular motion picture, *Master and Commander: The Far Side of the World*, featuring actor Russell Crowe. Among his many other accolades, Kennedy has the distinction of being the official artist for the annual Newport-to-Ensenada Yacht Race, the largest international event of its kind in the world.

Kennedy's ongoing love affair with the Baja California peninsula spans many decades, and he now makes his home in Baja Norte, where he overlooks the turquoise waters of La Bufadora cove on the Pacific

Artist Scott Kennedy takes a moment to relax under the hot Baja sun.
(MARIE-PIERRE)

coast. From there he can observe the pristine natural beauty that surrounds him, and sit upon his deck with either brush or pen in hand to carefully transfer his interpretation of what he feels and what he sees to canvas or paper.

He is presently in the process of completing two projects, one of which is a volume featuring compelling images of the tumultuous growth of Newport Harbor and adjoining coastal communities during the 1960s and 1970s. The other is a book of paintings and sketches retracing the steps of legendary writer John Steinbeck and his friend, Dr. Ed Ricketts. It depicts their epic journey around the entire coast of the Baja peninsula more than half a century ago, which is documented in Steinbeck's book, *The Log of the Sea of Cortez*.

One thing is certain: with Kennedy standing at the helm with pen and brush in hand, these two new ships are bound to sail as straight and keen a course as all the others he has artfully skippered for his many appreciative fans around the world.

Examples of Scott Kennedy's work can be found within the pages of this book, where he has deftly portrayed the spirit of each of the gamefish described (see Chapter 2).

For this vital contribution, I am eternally grateful.

Jonathan Schwartz

To some, Jonathan Schwartz is a mild-mannered Southern California schoolteacher who works diligently every day in the classroom while educating and enlightening the young minds entrusted to his charge. But to many others, he is also the noted kayak angler "Bluewater Jon," who travels the world in search of any big gamefish willing to attack and inhale his bait or lure as he patiently awaits their arrival from his sit-on-top kayak.

Bluewater Jon has traveled to some of the hottest areas in the world for large fish that other anglers would tackle only from behind the rail of a multilevel sport fishing cruiser. But despite the fact that he has fished the azure waters of Hawaii and the South Pacific, he is always drawn back to Baja California because of its unmatched proliferation of saltwater fish species.

In fact, he is so dedicated to this sport that he often hires a boat and skipper to take him and his kayak many miles offshore to pursue the coveted gamefish that have become his obsession. On one such adventure, while staying at the famous Punta Colorada Resort on Baja Sur's East Cape, Schwartz had an experience that he says he will never forget.

He relates, "I had my trusty pangero, René, take me and my 'yak on a twenty-minute boat ride south to the color break just off the lighthouse at the point. We had a tank that was full of live mullet, so I baited one up and paddled around for a few minutes until I got hammered by a quality-grade roosterfish, which I eventually landed and then quickly released."

Although he had been immediately successful, he soon found himself pulling around a live bait aimlessly and was almost beginning to wonder if there were any more hungry fish in the sea. But those thoughts were suddenly interrupted.

Schwartz continues: "After a little over twenty minutes of trolling, something grabbed my mullet and took off like a freight train! I tried to stop the fish, but soon realized that I was in for the fight of a lifetime. I mean, this fish tried everything in the book to get loose. I was being towed all over the place and kept looking back at René, who was following me with a big grin on his face.

"Well, about forty-five minutes later, I finally get it to the surface and it turns out to be another roosterfish, only this one's so huge that it's about three times the size of the one I had caught earlier. As soon as he got a look at me and the kayak he panicked, turned, quickly dove back into the depths, and then disappeared while once again, peeling off over fifty yards of line from my reel. It took me another ten minutes or so to get him back up."

But it turned out that Bluewater Jon was in for yet another surprise.

"Just like me, he seemed to be worn out and I was able to gently coax him over to the side of my 'yak so that René could take some photos while he was still in the water. I'm afraid that I had gotten a bit sidetracked by my battle with the big rooster, and didn't realize that he had towed me so close to the beach that I was now almost in the shore break.

"I heard René yell "Watch out!" but it was already too late. I was immediately hit by a wave and suddenly the fish and I were both floating in the water. My kayak was upside down and my rods, although tethered to its hull, were now dangling under the surface.

"Well, it was either rescue my rods, reels, and tackle or the roosterfish. This time I chose the fish. I grabbed him by the tail and started swimming behind him while pushing, and he seemed to respond; his featherlike dorsal fin was erect again and he looked for a moment like he was coming back to life. I, however, was getting extremely exhausted.

"I gave one last burst of effort and was finally able to get him up near the beach. By this time, both my 'yak and my rods and reels were strewn upside down in the sand like obstacles at Normandy Beach on D-Day. I remained committed to the fish, but it seemed as if he was slipping away and would not survive if I released him as first intended.

"I turned and looked out plaintively at René, who was still outside the breakers. Sadly, he gave me the hand-across-the-throat signal, indicating that the fish was a goner. I was subsequently released from doing any more work to try and revive the roosterfish without feeling guilty for abandoning him.

"Although this day had turned out to be rather expensive for me equipment-wise, I ended up feeling even worse about the death of such a fine roosterfish. It had not quite made it to be freed and to fight another day as I had originally planned.

"The roosterfish is usually released for sporting reasons, but also because it is not particularly prized as table fare. Their flesh is almost purple, like beef heart, and is very strong-tasting. Nonetheless, I vowed not to waste one scrap. I took him back to camp and, in the best Native American tradition, filleted him and eventually ate every bite."

Ivan Villarino

It is sometimes a bit of a surprise to English-speaking visitors to Vonny's Fleet panga camp in Punta Banda when they first encounter its owner, Ivan Villarino; although he is 100 percent "Mexicano puro," he communicates with the fluency of a native Southern Californian.

As a matter of fact, Ivan lived in Southern California for a number of years during his early youth. At least until he became old enough to realize that he couldn't stand all the congestion and wanted to return to a place where the pace of life is slower and cultural values are different.

He was also drawn back to his home in Punta Banda—a small poblado on northern Baja's Pacific coast at the southern end of Ensenada's Bahía de Todos Santos—because of his unabashed love of the sea. Villarino has been a skillful, instinctive, and highly focused angler all his life, and this is indeed a place where he can live out his passion in full measure.

The rich ocean waters nearby support an immense number of marine organisms, not the least of which are the wide varieties of popular gamefish species that are both migratory and territorial, and provide year-round angling opportunities.

Several decades ago, there were no reliable charter panga services anywhere in this fish-rich region. Anglers were left at the mercy of generally uncaring commercial pangeros, who didn't really give a hoot whether their customers caught fish or not. In fact, it was not uncommon for an unlucky group of anglers to get stuck with a hung-over skipper who was provided with only the bare minimum of gasoline that was perceived necessary to make the trip, which sometimes was not quite enough.

When Villarino first opened Vonny's Fleet many years ago, he named it after his daughter, Yvonne, and nurtured the fledgling business as if it were his youngest child.

Finally, after decades of frustration, visiting anglers had a place where they could get dependable panga charter service from an established, well-equipped, and highly knowledgeable outfitter.

He began with one 20-foot panga, which he skippered himself and launched right off the sandy beach near the end of the bay. Villarino, who is also a master mechanic and an innovative designer, even built his own "tilt-back" trailer to make it easier to retrieve his boats from the surf after he expanded his fleet. Ivan Villarino now owns four pangas and employs three full-time skippers to satisfy the demands of visiting anglers, who now fill his pangas in increasing numbers each season.

While Ivan rarely guides a trip himself these days, he's always ready to offer up one of his many tales relating to the exciting fishing experiences that he has enjoyed over the years off the coast of Ensenada.

Villarino recalls: "A few months after I originally opened Vonny's Fleet years ago, there was this customer of mine that kept saying he wanted me to take him out for a full day to fish for halibut exclusively. This was in early November, which is a bit late in the season, and I warned him that we might fish the whole darn trip and only catch a few halibut.

"That didn't bother him at all, so we set a date and launched off the beach on a nice day with calm seas. Well, it may have been pretty out on the water, but after a little over six hours of drifting with frozen anchovies we had only landed a few halibut, and none of them were over about two or three pounds; that was definitely not what we were out there for.

"Worse yet, we were running out of bait and only had a little over an hour left before we had to start heading back toward the beach. Talk about depressed, this poor guy was just staring off the starboard side into the water with a blank look on his face. It was killing me too, because I've always had a reputation for catching more than my share of halibut, and that is why he selected me to take him out that day.

"After the last bait was pinned on, I suggested that we give it one last try a little deeper and I moved us out into about sixty feet of water, a good depth for winter halibut. In addition to dropping the last anchovy down, I reached over near the outboard motor and picked up a small, dead mackerel that we had hooked inadvertently that morning. It was all dried out from the sun, but was still relatively fresh. After cutting a fillet-like flap from its tail to its belly, I 'mouse trap' rigged it with a live bait hook in the nose and a large treble hook in the tail and sent the eighteen-inch leader to the bottom along with a four-ounce torpedo sinker.

"'Oh, well. What did I expect comin' out here in November and tryin' to catch halibut; I'd say I was just a few months too late,'" My client offered with a sigh. "'Guess I should have had you take us out back in May after you first opened up!'"

"I was just about to apologize for not being able to put us on the fish this time, when the clicker on my reel started slowly ticking away and then got faster and faster. 'Looks like we got a taker on that stinky old mackerel!' I yelled over at him with a grin.

Although I had already set the hook, I was trying my best to nurse the fish to the boat because I wasn't sure how big he was, and we were only using seventeen-pound-test line. 'Do you want to take the pole?' I asked while trying to hand it off to him.

"'No, no,'" he quickly shot back. "'I want to take a picture if this turns out to be a big guy.'"

"Okay, that's your call," I replied. "But I really don't know if this is much bigger than twelve pounds or so."

"'That's all right,'" he responded. "'It's a hell of a lot bigger than anything that we've caught so far today.'"

"So I kept one eye on my line and one eye on the current to make sure that we kept the fish on the correct side of the boat. I kept cranking and lifting slowly, inching the fish in bit by bit.

"'Wow,'" remarked my client. "'This one looks like he might be even bigger than you thought.'"

"I tried not to pay attention because one false move might lose what we had been working all day for."

"'Good lord!'" he shouted, "'This guy is *huge!* Take a look down there!'"

"For the first time, I took my attention off the job at hand and looked over the rail of my panga. My blood ran cold; the big California halibut beneath the boat looked to be almost four feet long, with a giant fantail. But at this point in time he was just floating about a foot beneath the water's surface.

"Jeeez, we've got our hands full now!" I yelled while grabbing the large salmon landing net that I always have aboard. "Here, take the pole," I instructed. "Don't lift his head out of the water, and I'll net him.

"I slowly glided the big net up his body from behind and then quickly began to lift the big fish over the rail . . . but as soon as it felt itself coming out of the water, it bucked. And when it did, the handle of the net bent in half.

"My client alertly grabbed one side of the net's hoop and I grabbed the other as we lugged the giant halibut into the panga. I immediately picked up a belaying pin and smacked it over the noggin until it was fully subdued. A fish that size can do some serious damage once it's on your boat.

"It took us about twenty minutes to get back to shore, and my ecstatic client was smiling ear to ear every one of them. When we got back to my shop we put it on the scale. It weighed forty-five pounds, ten ounces.

"It's called 'fishing just for the halibut!'" Villarino added with a grin.

Gary Graham

Gary Graham was born in San Diego, California, and has been a prominent fixture on the Baja fishing scene for decades. He was named Angler of the Year by the National Coalition of Marine Conservation in 1987 and was appointed to a position as the Baja California representative for the International Game Fish Association (IGFA) in 1990. Graham has also written two books about fly fishing in Baja, including the *No Nonsense Guide to Southern Baja,* which is now in its second printing.

In the mid-1980s, Graham was one of the first to begin seriously fishing the East Cape beaches. Gary and his wife, Yvonne, the IGFA representative for Southern California own Baja on the Fly, a fly-fishing guiding and outfitting company. Along with their guides, they've hosted more than 2,000 fly-fishing clients in Baja Sur's East Cape region and other areas, including Cabo San Lucas, La Paz, Loreto, and Magdalena Bay. Graham is also a lifetime member of The Marlin Club of San Diego as well as The Tuna Club of Avalon on Catalina Island.

Recalling one his most satisfying Baja fishing excursions, Graham relates: "After spending a week fishing and photographing at Baja's East Cape beaches using our ATVs, Brian O'Keefe, world-renowned photographer, along with his wife and fishing partner Judith, had ticked most of the boxes. He had experienced outstanding fishing; we had caught roosters, jacks, pompano, and sierra from the beach with plenty of photos to prove it.

"As we sat on the porch of Rancho Deluxe watching the light fade and the purple darkness cloak Las Palmas Bay, Brian commented that he had never caught a snook, or 'robalo,' as they are called in Mexico. My thoughts immediately turned to Magdalena Bay and our conversation turned to snook.

"Ever since my first trip to Baja in the sixties I had heard many stories of snook in Baja, but they seemed to be more of a rumor than a documented fact. In the late nineties while researching my first book, *No Nonsense Guide to Fly Fishing Southern Baja,* Yvonne and I had gone to Magdalena Bay in search of legendary Baja snook. With little hard evidence of caught snook, I decided to hire Enrique Soto, one of the best pangeros in Puerto San Carlos, to take me into the esteros in search of the elusive snook.

"We also took Enrique's good buddy, Mario Muñoz, who fished for snook commercially. It turned out that Mario had been quite successful free-diving for the snook. After explaining to Mario that, as fly fishermen, we would release the snook that we caught, we convinced Mario to guide us into some of his favorite snook holes. For the next two days, Enrique and Mario took me from spot to spot. While I didn't catch any monsters, I did land a few snook on the fly. More importantly, I had the opportunity to observe the habitat that seemed to be the most productive.

"Since Brian and Judith had a few days remaining in Baja before they would be returning to their home in Oregon, I suggested that we make a quick trip to Puerto San Carlos and see if we could find Brian and Judith their first Baja snook.

"Early the next morning, Don Sloan, my fishing partner, and I met Brain and Judith on Highway 1 to begin another Baja adventure. Midday we arrived in Puerto San Carlos, and Enrique Soto was waiting for us at Hotel Brennan. Enrique was ready with his panga in the water and it only took a few minutes to load our gear.

"Streaking across the bay to one of my favorite snook spots, I went over the basics that I had learned about Baja snook with both Brian and Judith. Sliding to a stop in the narrow, mangrove-lined channel, I pointed at a likely looking hole nearly covered by overhanging brush. Brian was first up and cast his fly perfectly into the spot where I pointed.

"Immediately he began rapidly stripping the fly. After several casts, I suggested that he let the fly sink for a five count, allowing the fly to be swept out into the channel halfway through the retrieve. Brian set the hook as the snook inhaled the fly. Loose line began flying off the deck as Brian frantically tried to keep it from tangling until it was taut against the spool.

"The snook tried to return to its lair among the stumps, but Brian held on and slowly turned the fish, bringing it back to the boat. Brian's first Baja snook was landed after a few casts and less than an hour after he began fishing the esteros! Needless to say, we all celebrated that night while making our plans for the next day.

"The late, legendary Fred Hoctor, author of *Baja Ha Ha* and Baja columnist for *Western Outdoor News* until his untimely passing several years ago, had given me some vague information about a hidden estero at the southern end of the bay, his 'secret hot snook spot.' As the sun turned the sky blood red the next morning, we punched it for Fred's secret spot.

"We traveled over fifty miles in the panga but we couldn't find the opening to Fred's estero. In desperation, we went even farther, only to turn back a few hours later. As we retraced our way back, our luck held and we spotted a couple of Mexican kids pushing their old panga through a shallow opening. Making a quick left, we headed for that opening.

"The tide was up just enough for us to enter the small estero. We slowly made our way into the channel, with me standing watch on the bow, looking down into water clear enough for me to see all the way to the bottom. Among the stumps along the bank, I spotted large numbers of grouper, pargo, and snook stacked like cordwood. We had found Fred's secret spot.

"It was easy for Don and Brian to wade and cast into the deep part of the channel from a shallow sandbar on the opposite side across from the cache of fish. For the next several hours, almost every cast was a bite. By the time the tide had reached flood stage, we all were whipped and happy. After a long ride uphill, it was another night of celebration as we toasted Fred Hoctor and his 'secret spot' that had provided some incredible nonstop action for pargo, grouper, and snook up to twenty pounds.

"Later, I called Fred to thank him for giving me the tip that, when coupled with some high-tech satellite imagery and the help of two Mexican kids, had led us to one of my most memorable Magdalena Bay adventures."

Denis Quesnel

Southern California resident Denis Quesnel has been hooked on fishing the waters of Baja California for decades. More than 30 years ago, he and other members of the Orange Coast Rod & Gun Club began fishing in Baja and ended up becoming regular passengers on panga

Denis Quesnel of Action Lures shows off one the quality kelp bass available in and around Baja Norte's prolific kelp forests. (ACTION LURES)

motherships based out of San Felipe that fish for up to six days at a time. They made a point to take these trips every season that they could and, over the years, caught countless numbers of big yellowtail, snapper, grouper, and white sea bass adjacent to the many small islands that are scattered just off the coast of the upper Sea of Cortez.

Quesnel became so immersed in the sport that he eventually designed and began manufacturing a new generation of iron jigs. His Action Lures are jointed two-thirds of the way down the body so that they will still dance enticingly while being jigged up and down in the vast and sometimes notoriously deep caverns of the Sea of Cortez.

Denis Quesnel has since become a regular seasonal guest on The Outdoor Channel's *American Outdoorsman* television show, and has accompanied its host, Mark Tobin, and his crew to fishing hotspots around the Baja peninsula for a shot at popular gamefish of practically every description.

Back in the early days, however, Quesnel and his buddies were trying to figure out a way to conserve their stamina in the region's intense heat during June and July, which also happens to be the most productive time to fish the Sea of Cortez. In its northern realm, daytime temperatures during these times are frequently in the triple digits, and can sometimes reach over 112 degrees. Jigging a heavy lure up and down for several hours in these conditions is not only exhausting—the brutal heat can sap your soul of every bit of the enthusiasm that it took to go on such a fishing trip in the first place.

One weekend while he was at home puttering around in his garage, Denis got the idea to cut a metal, candy bar-style jig in half and then rejoin the two pieces together with a sturdy stainless steel ring. After doing so he tied it to a piece of fishing line and tossed it into his swimming pool. As he jerked it along the bottom, he immediately noticed how its "broken-back" action flashed erratically through the water like a wounded baitfish without very much effort on his part. He instinctively felt that he might be onto something, and vowed to take it along to try out on his next multiday panga trip in Baja.

The rest is pretty much history. Quesnel relates: "On the first day of our trip that next summer, we were in one of the pangas fishing off San Francisquito just south of Bahía de Los Angeles, the sun was already blazing, and it felt like it had to be well over 100 degrees.

"There were a lot of forage fish in the water that day, and no one onboard any of the other boats was catching very much on live bait; the fish wouldn't touch our conventional iron jigs either. I looked in my tackle box, took out my homemade lure, and decided that this was the time to give it a shot.

He continues: "Call it beginner's luck, but on my very first drop I only had to give it a twitch or two before my rod was practically jerked from my hands as something very big proceeded to bend my pole in half as it started peeling line off my reel. I very carefully tightened the drag just a bit to make him have to work harder to try and spool me and, after about twenty minutes, he eventually succumbed to fatigue and came to color.

The fish turned out to be a sweet 30-pound yellowtail, and by the end of the day Quesnel had used his hand-fashioned lure to boat two more yellows of similar size. Anglers on the other pangas, however, had not been so fortunate and caught only a few small miscellaneous species that they had not actually been targeting.

Denis Quesnel suddenly realized that he was onto something.

After returning home from the trip, Quesnel began working feverishly in his garage to make as many of the lures as possible, first to share with other members of his fishing club, and eventually to sell. After several years in business, crewmembers aboard local sport fishing boats began to notice the higher fish counts of anglers using the jigs, and sales began to soar.

Although he has since fished in many regions around the entire Baja peninsula, one of Quesnel's most memorable fishing adventures took place in the upper regions of the Sea of Cortez. While aboard a mothership panga near Punta Final, north of Bahía de Los Angeles, he encountered a white sea bass bite that he will never forget.

Quesnel relates: "I had never caught a big white sea bass before, and we had just stopped briefly at a new spot very close to shore to try and catch a few cabrilla. All of a sudden the water next to our panga exploded with a giant boil at the surface, and then another . . . and another! After a split second of being totally awestruck, everyone onboard began casting live baits and iron jigs into the middle of the wild melee, and the rods all started going 'bendo' practically simultaneously. Everybody was catching fish, but my homemade lure was really nailing them because, while it had the action of live bait, I never had to take the time to grab another sardina from the bait tank and pin it on the hook. I just kept swinging them over the rail and then was almost immediately able to cast out again.

"When we eventually decided to leave the spot, we did so not because the bite was over—we simply had too many big fish onboard to safely carry any more. When the smoke finally cleared I had caught a total of thirty-three white sea bass, each weighing over twenty pounds.

"Not only did that day's catch end up providing our dinner table with delicate sea bass fillets for literally months on end, it was also one of the most exciting and productive days on the water that I have ever spent."

Jeff deBrown

The sport of saltwater fly fishing has grown increasingly popular over the past 10 years, and nowhere is this phenomenon more apparent than on the East Cape of Baja California Sur. These days, many of the anglers who visit here are more interested in casting a fly to a 20-pound roosterfish than in heading offshore in a cruiser and trolling around with a colorfully feathered jethead for 200-pound striped marlin.

For those anglers, Jeff deBrown, who also happens to be one of the only Orvis-certified fly-fishing guides in Baja, offers a decided advantage to those first-timers, and even to veterans who could use a few professional pointers to help them get the job done.

The Reel Baja, deBrown's company, caters to the needs of his clients throughout the Los Cabos to La Paz corridor, but he spends most of his time guiding anglers who are staying at well-known East Cape resorts including Hotel Buena Vista, Rancho Leonero, and Punta Colorada.

Although he has literally hundreds of memories of great days on the water with his customers and friends, there is one in particular that often comes to mind.

Says deBrown: "Over the years, I have had the opportunity to guide many fine anglers as well as help them to catch a fish that fits into what they feel is the 'fish of a lifetime.' None, however, stands out in my mind like the day I had off Baja Sur fly fishing for marlin with my client Brian Crawford from New Mexico.

"Shortly after he was scheduled to check in at Rancho Leonero, I dropped by the hotel to introduce myself. I also wanted to find out if there was any particular type of fishing that he would like to focus on, since this was his first trip to Baja, and the first time he had ever done any fly fishing in salt water. He wasn't in his room, and down here in the late afternoon it is often a safe bet that many guests will find themselves near the pool, cocktail lounge, or both.

"After approaching the outside patio, I scanned the area for what

Orvis-certified fly-fishing guide Jeff deBrown (right) gasps in delight as his client lands his fish of a lifetime while fishing offshore near Baja Sur's famed East Cape region. (THE REEL BAJA)

one might think of as a typical fly-fishing angler with the long-billed hat, polarized sunglasses hanging around their neck, and a multi-pocketed fishing shirt. But all I saw was a guy sitting at one of the tables who looked like he would be more at home riding a Harley-Davidson down the street at the Sturgis motorcycle festival.

"I walked over to the table where the big, burly man sat and, with some hesitation, asked, 'Brian?'

"He quickly turned around toward me with one of the biggest grins on his face that I have ever seen and responded, 'Jeff?'

"After sitting down at his table, we talked for quite a while and I learned that Brian was actually an eighth-grade science teacher who had been saving his money for over five years to come down and go fly fishing on the East Cape. During our conversation, he also told me that over most of those years he kept dreaming of catching a marlin on a fly rod. Brian then added that he had watched every video, read every article, and watched every television show that he could find about fly fishing for marlin.

"While staring off into the distance, he paused and then remarked, 'Yeah. Catching a marlin on a fly rod is my perfect dream.'

"Without missing a beat, I optimistically offered, 'Well, we've had lots of striped marlin in the area lately. How about starting out first thing tomorrow morning to see if we can't make that dream come true?'

"After arriving at the hotel the next morning, I found Brian sitting right where he was the previous afternoon. We had a quick breakfast, but before we had finished he asked me one more time, 'We are really going to fish for marlin today, right?'

"I assured him with a grin that, indeed, we were. After boarding our panga, we headed out toward the fishing grounds. I quickly learned that I really didn't have to explain very much to Brian regarding where he should cast, how to set the hook, or about any other aspect of fly fishing for marlin. After all, he had five long years of research under his belt and simply needed to find a fish to try out his acquired knowledge.

"We eventually reached one of the areas that had been producing stripers over the past few weeks and, after putting a few teasers in the water and making a few practice casts, we were ready to catch some fish.

"This day, things got going right out of the gate and, after only about ten minutes or so of pulling around the teasers, the skipper and I found ourselves shouting, almost in unison, 'Marlin! Marlin! Marlin!'

"Brian grabbed his fly rod as I grabbed the teasing pole and started to lure the fish within casting distance of the boat while yelling to him: 'Get ready, get ready . . . get ready!'

"Brian kept pressing, 'Now? Now?'

"Not yet!" I said, "Not yet . . . hold on . . . *Now!*' I commanded.

"Like a poised viper waiting to strike, Brian suddenly lashed forth with a cast that was, in a word, perfect. The big billfish couldn't resist, and immediately streaked over to the fly, quickly inhaled it, and then shot off into the blue.

"Brian kept yelling, 'Can I set the hook now? Can I set the hook? Please?!' and then gave me a look like I was going to let his dream fish escape. Actually, I just wanted to make sure that the marlin had fully taken the fly. Almost immediately, the fish was at the perfect angle. 'Nail him!' I shouted. 'Set the hook!'

"That's all Brian was waiting for. He set the hook with every ounce of strength he had in his huge, hulking frame. And, as he did, his dream marlin suddenly leaped out of the water and proceeded to tail-walk on the surface for nearly 300 yards.

"Brian was in heaven, and kept shouting out, 'Look, look . . . I have a *marlin* on!'

"After about twenty more minutes, and many jumps and line-peeling runs, Brian had the marlin at the boat and ready to land. I reached down and grabbed the bill of the marlin and pulled it over the side as our skipper, Santos, snapped photos of us with my camera.

"I asked Brian to remove the fly and, as he did, I could tell that he was overcome with emotion. We lowered the big fish back into the water, and Brian released his bill, gave him a big push, and the marlin slowly began meandering away from the boat. He watched it eventually disappear into the deep purple-blue of the Sea of Cortez, and then turned to look at me with tears streaming down his face.

"'Thank you,' he softly croaked. 'After dreaming about this moment for five years, it was perfect. It was just perfect! Thank you!'

"At this point, we both needed a little time to reflect upon the events and epiphanies of the day that had provided both my client and me with many thoughts to ponder. Neither of us said much on the way back to the dock, but we didn't have to; we were both immensely satisfied."

As an epilogue to his tale, deBrown adds, "Most of us who guide professionally do so for different reasons, but few of us ever delude ourselves into thinking that we are likely to become millionaires in this business. Personally, I happen to be a Baja fishing guide because I believe that, hopefully, I can regularly contribute in some small way to making an angler's 'perfect dream' come true. And every time I'm able to accomplish that goal, it makes me feel like a millionaire!"

Capt. Kelly Catian

Capt. Kelly Catian is a fortunate man. He and his family are able to live their lives next to the rich, picturesque waters of Bahía San Quintín on Baja's Pacific coast. This famous bay provides many good reasons for both anglers and hunters to pay a seasonal visit to what has become a prime recreational paradise. Its meandering canals, long sandy beaches, excellent fishing both inside and outside the bahía, and the yearly migration of black brant to the area offer year-round opportunities for outdoor adventure.

Along with his partner, Monte Kotur, who lives in Southern

Expert skipper and fish finder Capt. Kelly Catian gives the victory sign after another successful day on the water (TOM GATCH)

California, Catian owns and operates K&M Sportfishing, and is the administrator of their active fleet of five high-end fishing boats. The mini-armada includes a 28-foot Amato and a 25-foot Parker, each equipped with a pilothouse, a 23-foot Parker cuddy cabin, and two 26-foot super pangas. By regional standards, this makes their sport fishing operation one of the most prominent anywhere along the Baja Norte coast south of Ensenada.

But this was not always the case.

In 1985, native Southern Californian Kelly Catian was just another laid-back surfer living in San Clemente. Like many others, he often spent many warm, sunny days riding the local waves, partying, and also trying to figure out what he really wanted to do with the rest of his life. Shortly before, his parents had moved down to San Quintin to live in semi-retirement while his father, Don Jorge, operated what was then the only tackle shop in this remote locale.

The next year, during a telephone conversation with his father, Catian expressed confusion regarding his long-term goals. His father quickly suggested that he take a short sabbatical and stay with them down in San Quintin for a while to do a little fishing and sort things out. Kelly took him up on the invitation and, as it turns out, he has never crossed the northern border back into the United States again, except as a temporary visitor.

Not too long after arriving and staying at his parents' home in San Quintin, he met his future wife, Bertha, with whom he eventually raised three boys, Oscar, George, and Christian. Oscar now skippers one of the charter boats, and George is set to be next in line. He and his sons are all avid free-divers and surfers as well, and regularly take advantage of the world-class swells that encroach upon their coastline during the winter months.

Says Catian: "Back when we first started out, there were no fish finders and no GPS units . . . I learned to navigate using a compass mounted on half a foam buoy and a wristwatch, that was it!" He adds: "It wasn't easy. There were some rough years where we lived pretty much off of the ocean. We didn't have many clients then, maybe three a month. The rest of the time I had to do commercial fishing and diving to make ends meet."

Luckily, Catian's innate talent for finding fish, along with his dogged tenacity, eventually earned him a reputation with many visiting anglers as the guy to go out fishing with in San Quintin. But, after joining forces with his new partner, things really began to take off as they acquired their collection of sleek, pilothouse-equipped Parker cruisers that were capable of getting farther offshore much quicker than their local competition, which was limited by their markedly slower conventional pangas.

Over the years, he has had many exciting days out on the water, but says that there is one trip that is particularly well etched into his memory.

Recalls Catian: "It was in October of 2006. We had been booking back-to-back charters all summer long, and we finally got the chance to take a few days off to go out and have some fun late in the month.

"There was supposed to by a nice swell coming in from a hurricane way down south, and my son, Oscar, and his buddy, Charky, were already down off Socorro Beach a few miles south of the entrada getting in on the action with their surfboards.

"It was one of those classic Baja mornings—a clear sunny sky, and warm deep-blue water. We tore out of the mouth of the bay at about 39+ knots over glassy seas, and finally pulled up outside the reef where Oscar and Charky were busily riding waves. My co-owner, Monte Kotur, was also onboard along with K&M crewmembers, Dave Brown and Chris Pierce.

"I remember that it was only about nineteen feet deep at the edge of the reef where we were sitting when I grabbed one of our surfboards and was getting ready to jump into the water to catch a few waves. Suddenly, a huge, dark shadow passed under the boat, then another . . . and another. For a split second, I stood there stunned by the fact that I was looking down at a school of some of the biggest white sea bass that I had ever seen before; most of the fish appeared to be well over fifty pounds.

"Then the screaming started.

"Everyone was scrambling over the surfboards trying to grab their fishing pole and get a jig tied on. Dave Brown was the first to get hit, and wasn't even able to get 'I'm *on!*' completely out of his mouth before line started rapidly peeling off his reel.

"'Me too!' yelled Monte Kotur immediately thereafter while, a heartbeat later, Chris Pierce shouted 'Got him!' as his pole bent in half and his reel began to scream. The fact was we were now *all* hooked up simultaneously with incredibly large sea bass, which were even bigger than we first thought; the first one over the rail weighed over seventy pounds.

"It was pandemonium. We were all scurrying around trying to follow our line and land the freshest fish we had on while stepping over the ones between fifty and seventy pounds that had already hit the deck. After an almost timeless interlude of this frenzied action, the tide had risen and the fish were suddenly gone, but so was the big surf.

"We all sat bleary-eyed, a few of us clutching cold cervezas, as we surveyed the fish scattered on the deck before us. Our bountiful catch would later yield us a couple hundred pounds of gourmet-quality fillets after being cleaned and processed back at the dock.

"As I rested a few more minutes in contemplation of our incredible, unexpected catch of a lifetime, I came to the conclusion that it was just as well that we never got to ride those nearly perfect offshore breaks. After all, if we came back with a story of both fantastic surfing *and* a record-breaking catch of white sea bass all on the same trip, it's likely that no one would have believed us anyway."

Dennis Spike

It's not that Dennis Spike invented the practice of fishing from a kayak. He had, after all, been beaten to the punch by various aboriginal tribes several thousand years ago. But, having said that, he would certainly have to be considered one of the pioneers in the development and promotion of the sit-on-top kayak fishing craze that we see going on these days.

It was long before anyone had given much thought to the idea that the newly marketed plastic kayaks of the late 1980s and early 1990s were anything much more than adult toys that were most appropriately used at bayside picnics. Traditional kayakers eschewed them because riders sat on top of, rather than inside, the craft. They looked slow and clumsy on the water, had no skirts, and relied solely upon scupper holes to get rid of unwanted water. Some critics even described them as being downright dangerous.

Nonetheless, Dennis Spike, a dedicated angler who at the time had no boat of his own, couldn't help but be intrigued by the prospect of this new, low-budget way to get into some of the great inshore fishing that was available just off Malibu Beach.

Spike recalls: "My cousin and I started rigging up our open-top kayaks for fishing and, from day one, each of our trips was consistently better than the previous one. My first year in a kayak, I fished over 150 times in areas that were otherwise accessed almost exclusively by powerboats . . . and caught more fish than I ever had before."

He kept refining his technique and, over time, Spike became one of the most recognized and readily acknowledged diehards connected to the sport of kayak fishing on the California coast. What was originally his passion for fishing and the outdoors suddenly turned into a career change when his first feature article on kayak fishing appeared in *Pacific Fisherman* magazine, then a popular West Coast sport fishing publication.

Since that time, his company, Coastal Kayak Fishing, has helped supply and guide literally hundreds of new and veteran kayak anglers with seminars and supervised trips to exotic, out-of-the-way locations in Southern California and Baja. Dennis Spike is also the resident kayak fishing guide at one of Baja Sur's most popular East Cape resorts, Rancho Leonero. During his tenure there, Spike has regularly encountered fishing experiences that many other anglers only dream of.

He remembers: "I was guiding a group of very experienced kayak fishermen out of the ranch, and we were in a fairly tight group about a mile from shore. We were particularly lucky that morning; there was plenty of quality bait onboard the cruiser that we use as our mothership, and the fish in the area were definitely on the chew. Before long we were catching dorado up to twenty pounds, and some yellowfin tuna a little smaller than that."

While most of the live baits were sardinas, there was also a caballito in the tank, which is a larger baitfish that is actually a member of the jack family. Spike decided to give it a shot with the bigger bait, and pinned the nervous fish to his hook.

The cruiser's skipper, René, who also happened to be one of the resort's top captains, looked down at Dennis Spike and, with an ominous tone in his voice said, "You gonna catch a sailfish." It was as if he was playfully suggesting that Spike wouldn't be able to handle such a challenge from his relatively small kayak.

But, in an effort to seem nonchalant, Spike casually responded, "Oh, that's okay," as he glanced up at the captain with a devilish grin.

As the official guide, however, he could not afford to neglect his clients in order to catch fish on his own; immediately after live-lining out his bait he became embroiled in helping one of the kayakers get a difficult backlash out of his reel. He practically forgot that he even had a bait out.

Without warning, he suddenly felt the back of his kayak shake aggressively and quickly turned to see his rod bend double and, with its butt still firmly in the rod holder, watched its tip dip below the surface of the water. At the same time, line began tearing off his reel as if the other end was attached to a freight train.

As he pulled the rod from the holder, the line just as suddenly went slack. Reeling frantically, he wasn't really sure if the fish had come unbuttoned, had broken off, or was heading toward him.

In the next moment his question was answered, as one of the other anglers began yelling, "Look! It's . . . a *sailfish*!" Spike felt as if someone had just slugged him in the gut, but kept on cranking, knowing that it was now vitally important that he get as much of that slack line as possible back onto his reel.

By the time he was able to get control of the big sailfish, it had already made numerous jumps in the direction of his kayak, and then unexpectedly burst up past the surface less than 6 feet from where he sat. It was at this very second that Dennis realized that, like several other unfortunate fishermen, he could easily be impaled by the fish's giant bill, with fatal consequences. But fortunately, that last jump turned out to be the last one the great fish made before tearing off downcurrent, towing Spike's kayak behind it.

"It was quite a ride," he recalls. "René kept yelling at me to keep the line tight, but he didn't have to—I already had the drag hammered down so that the fish would hopefully tire out a little quicker; we *really* wanted to avoid killing it."

And that is exactly what happened. The fatigued sailfish finally came submissively alongside his kayak.

Spike adds: "Two of the other kayakers who were in a tandem boat came over as I removed my hook from the fish's mouth with my pliers. I then held the sailfish by its tail with both hands as they began to slowly tow me backward so that we could force water through the gills of the exhausted fish.

"After a few minutes of our attempts to revive it, I felt his tail twitch and then quickly slap back in the other direction. I released my grasp, and we all watched this magnificent creature disappear back into the deep blue waters of the Cortez to a hearty round of applause by everyone present."

Then, Dennis reminisced with a somewhat distant gaze: "Yeah, that's the big one that we all really wanted to get away."

Jonathan Roldan

After Jonathan Roldan, Esq. received his Juris Doctor degree and began practicing law in Southern California, it didn't take long for him to realize that, although he had achieved what modern American society might refer to as "success," there was still something missing.

As time progressed, this became even more apparent when he found himself dealing with many dishonest or disreputable individuals on practically a daily basis. Eventually, he began to sort things out and finally determined what was missing from his well- structured career and urban lifestyle: it was passion.

Many who come to this realization dutifully suppress the desire to embrace change and plunge into the uncertain. But Roldan, who had always been a dedicated angler, jumped on an opportunity to relocate to the beautiful city of La Paz on the east coast of Baja Sur to manage a sport fishing and diving guide service. That was several years ago, and he has never looked back.

Today, he operates Tailhunter International, a premier outfitter for on-the-water adventures in this popular tourist region. Jonathan Roldan is also a writer and columnist for *Western Outdoor News,* one of the nation's largest weekly fishing and hunting publications.

When asked to single out one of his most exciting moments fishing the clear blue subtropical waters off La Paz, Roldan offers: "There are times when you just know that you're in trouble, and this was one of them. Big trouble . . . a 'seeing your life flash before your eyes' kind of trouble!"

"This client of mine, Tom, had brought groups of his buddies down to La Paz on several occasions over the years to fish with my guide service, and he was a great person to deal with. This trip, the guys had enjoyed a few banner days of fishing around nearby Cerralvo Island. A few had picked up billfish, but there was also an outstanding bite of nice yellowfin tuna at the northwest side of the island.

"Now, unless you've ever tangled with a member of the tuna family, you have no idea of the power of these fish. They're built like a streamlined football, packed with muscle, and blessed with the ability to dive fast and swim at bursts of speed up to 50 miles per hour, they are arguably the toughest fish, pound for pound, in the entire ocean.

"As I often explain to my fishing clients, catching marlin of two hundred, three hundred, heck, even up to over a thousand pounds has been done. But no one has yet been able to put a four-hundred-pound ahi on the deck with a rod and reel, and even three-hundred-pound fish are rare.

"For the past three days, these clients had been catching some nice fifty-pound yellowfin tuna, which had basically amounted to hour-long slugfests between man and fish. Everyone had brought several tuna onboard . . . except for Tom.

"Don't get me wrong, Tom's a good angler, but this just didn't seem to be his week. Several times, he had been busted off or hooks had pulled out. Another time, a passing panga had cut him off. It was just sheer, dumb, bad luck. Tom was snakebit and, although he was grinning through it all, I couldn't let the charter master get goose-egged with no fish.

"So, there we were on the last day of fishing. I had agreed to personally guide for him, which put a big smile on his face. He was a good sport, and loved that his guys were having a great time, but enough was enough! It was showtime.

"Luckily, this trip was the one where things turned out a bit different for Tom. The fishing was red hot right out of the chute; the first bait to hit the water was immediately inhaled by one of a pack of hungry yellowfin tuna that ended up bending his rod in half. 'Oh, yeah!' Tom grinned over at me. 'This is more like it!' he shouted.

"But about ten minutes later, zing, powie! The line snapped with a loud pop. Here we go again, I thought, as Tom's smile suddenly turned upside down.

"Okay, another hook, another bait. We flylined off the starboard side and *whoosh!* Another hook-up! Grins all around.

"Come on, Tom," I silently whined. "You gotta bust the curse with this one!

"But no! Half an hour later, the hook just came unbuttoned! This was no good; the score was now fish two, anglers zero.

"And so it went. As other boats around us hooked and landed, we went through two more solid hook-ups that, for no apparent reason, just, what can I say, fell out! Talk about being jinxed.

"Worse, it was now getting pretty late. We had hooked and fought four fish, but had zero to show for it. Tom was being a good sport about it, saying 'That's fishing,' with a shrug, but I knew he was as frustrated as all get out, just like a home run hitter who starts doubting himself during a bad stretch.

"Last bait.

"A silent prayer from both of us with a nervous laugh and once again, *fish on!* This one looked solid. It was up and down, back and forth for almost forty-five minutes. This time, Tom had skillfully put the wood to the tuna.

"Then, out of the corner of my eye, I caught a glimpse of another panga heading straight toward Tom's line. 'No!' I yelled. 'Stop! You're gonna . . .'

"Fortunately, the captain saw me waving my arms and was able to stop in time, but something was very wrong. Tom's rod was still bent, but the situation was not good. His line was now tangled in the outboard prop of the other panga, which was drifting over thirty yards away! Its captain tried desperately to untangle the line, but with no success. Something was hanging it up.

"I looked around and thought 'Oh . . . what the hell.' Off came my shirt, and I dove into the water. I don't usually do things like that, but we just couldn't lose this fish!

"I free-stroked over to the other boat and was just about there when I heard Tom groan and swear! I looked back. His rod was no longer bent. It was standing straight up and unloaded. I could see that the line had apparently cut.

"We lost the fish. My heart sank.

"Well, there wasn't very much that we could do at this point in the trip. We wouldn't have time to go outside again, and there was an awful lot of line out that Tom had mentioned was brand new. A quick duck under the water and I easily freed the line from around the prop.

"'Ni modo,' (can't be helped) he said with a shrug of apology for the lost fish.

"I agreed. Oh well. That's fishing. It was an accident. I figured I'd swim back to our own panga and wrap the line up when I got back into the boat. I took the loose end of the line, wound it around my wrist, and started to swim back toward our boat where Tom and our own skipper were waiting.

"Suddenly my arm shot out away from me in a violent tug, and it felt as if it was going to be yanked out of the socket as I was quickly pulled underwater. Time seemed to stand still as I came to the jarring realization that Tom's tuna was *still* attached to the line, and that line was now wrapped around my wrist and was pulling me beneath the surface.

"I frantically kicked my way up again and screamed 'Bring the boat! Bring the boat! The tuna is still on the line!' I was treading water as best I could while our panga moved closer, and other boats began coming in to see what all the screaming and thrashing was about.

"I hollered out for them to strip out some loose line. I could feel my heart racing as I got next to the gunwale of the panga and told our skipper to grab my leg and swing it over. Once again, my head got pulled under as I fought to stay above the water.

"With my leg hooked over the low-lying gunwale, I yelled for someone to give me the end of Tom's line. It seemed like it took forever, but I managed to get a little slack on the line with the tuna and do a quick splice.

"I called over to Tom: 'When I let go, you reel like hell!' I could see his eyes widen to the size of silver dollars. 'Here we go. One . . . two . . . three!' I let go.

"Immediately, Tom began cranking furiously and suddenly, mercifully, his rod bent in half and his reel began screaming as the big tuna ripped of line. 'Yeah!' he shrieked with the zeal of a delighted child on Christmas morning. 'Fish on!'

"Meanwhile, my skipper managed to pull me aboard to the applause and cheers of half a dozen boats and friends of Tom who had also gathered around. I collapsed on the deck to catch my breath and then, after a few seconds, stood up.

"Tom was still firmly on the fish and was now laughing and shouting, 'That's service! Now *that* is service!'

"After being gaffed and brought aboard, Tom's yellowfin tuna ended up weighing out at just over sixty pounds.

"When we got back to the beach, I received a generous tip and the sweetest-tasting beer that I have ever enjoyed. But a few hours later, after the excitement of the moment had a chance to dissipate, I found myself feeling quite fortunate for having changed my career path several years ago. Because, as electrifying as the events of the day had been, for me it was just another day at the office in Baja."

Rick Roessler

Rick Roessler, a veteran video production specialist and author of the popular DVDs *Fun Flying Baja* and *Fun Driving Baja*, is also a longtime Baja bush pilot who has, at one time or another, flown one of his small airplanes over virtually every inch of the Baja California peninsula.

"Baja Ricky," as he is known to his many friends, is not only a pilot who is masterfully adept at controlling his own private aircraft, he is also an expert mechanic who dismantles, examines, repairs if necessary, and then reassembles his plane on an annual basis in compliance with FAA regulations.

"Baja Ricky" Roessler, ready to hit the sky. (RICK ROESSLER)

Roessler has been known to briefly set his small, red-and-white Cessna down on a remote Baja beach that is miles from civilization to casually adjust or fix just about any aspect of the plane's operation that he is not comfortable with. He will then, just as languidly, get back into the cockpit, buzz down the sand, and lift off into the clear blue Baja sky on the way to his original destination.

Needless to say, if you are going to have a problem in the sky over Baja, there's probably no better guy to have at your side than Rick Roessler. His good buddy, Greg Finley, can personally attest to that fact.

In mid-April 2005, he and Roessler planned a two-plane excursion down the eastern coast of Baja to the pleasantly isolated area of San Franscisquito, which lies just below Bahía de Los Angeles near the frontier between Baja Norte and Baja Sur.

Roessler would carry his friend, Ted Nestor, in his 1962 red-and-white Cessna Skylark, while Finley would pilot his 1970 Piper Cherokee with copilot Bob Gabhart, who, with his 800-plus hours of flying time, had even more experience in the air than Finley did. It was a trip that was well planned and involved only individuals who knew exactly how to handle themselves when flying at well over 100 miles per hour just a few thousand feet above the ground.

The weather was gorgeous, and a few hours after taking off from Gillespie Field in San Diego County, the two airplanes were cruising calmly over the stunningly beautiful waters of the Sea of Cortez.

Gabhart recalls: "We saw whales sunning themselves, fleets of pelicans flying in formation, and dolphins chasing mackerel, which were chasing something else farther down the food chain. The air was calm, and the water was deep blue and glassy."

But, less than a half hour from their destination, while traveling over the breathtaking natural harbor of Bahía de Los Angeles and its many small, picturesque islands, something quite unusual occurred.

Remembers Bob Gabhart: "It was the most sickening sound that you could imagine hearing in an airplane. It was a sound that jolted me from a mindset of pleasurable sightseeing to one of adrenaline-induced panic. This was the legendary effect that slows motion and makes time elastic.

The loud pop that he had heard was followed immediately by a violent shaking of the aircraft. It was so intense that both men were terrified that the plane might break apart at any moment. The cockpit suddenly began to fill with crankcase and oil fumes as they noticed, to their horror, that the propeller had stopped dead in its tracks—the engine had apparently seized up.

Being the more experienced of the two, Gabhart immediately took over the controls, got on the radio, and exclaimed, "Mayday! *Mayday!* Ricky, we're going in!" Then he suddenly realized that he had just taken on the job description of a glider pilot.

He offers: "I'll never say that any part of this ordeal was fun by any means," then adds, "But, in some part of my adrenaline-charged mind, flying that airplane down to the water was absolutely amazing!"

In a split second, the craft hit the water and flipped onto its back as water quickly rushed into the cabin and the men desperately did their best to free themselves from the rapidly sinking airplane.

Meanwhile, circling above them, Rick Roessler and his passenger, Ted, had been on top of the situation from the moment they heard Bob's mayday call over the radio. They were eventually able to drop two life vests down to Greg and Bob, who were now treading water and moving away from the jettisoned Cherokee as quickly as possible. Unfortunately, the men in the water saw only one of the vests, but that was enough. They immediately created a human life raft between them while one paddled and the other kicked toward shore.

Roessler put out another general mayday call, literally praying that someone would hear him and promptly respond to his plea. Because of the direction of the current and the prevailing winds, he realized that the two were much too far from shore to ever make it by themselves. It was then that he came to what he later described as one of the toughest decisions he has ever made in his entire life: whether or not to leave his friends in an attempt to find some help and ultimately save their lives.

He soon came to the conclusion that there was no other rational choice than to do exactly that.

Bahía de Los Angeles is not only a popular destination for recreational anglers, but also has several commercial panga operations as well. Roessler felt that his only hope might be to reach one of the local fish camps and then enlist the emergency assistance of a few of the pangeros to go out and try to find his friends before it was too late.

After recalling seeing an encampment that they had flown over a few minutes before the Cherokee began having problems, he started heading in that direction. Shortly, a tiny, dusty runway came into view and Roessler expertly laid his little Cessna right in the middle of it.

Rick and Ted hurriedly jumped from the plane and began running up the dirt road to the fish camp about a mile and a half away. It was only a few moments, however, before they were treated to the merciful sight of a four-wheel-drive ATV driving down the path in their direction.

The two people on the ATV were visiting Canadians and, as soon as they found out what was going on, the four of them were speeding back toward the panga camp. Once there, the fleet captain quickly grabbed a 5-gallon gas can and had one of the pangas launched so that he and Ted could head out on the water, while Rick returned to his airplane and tried to relocate his two friends from the sky.

After some time in the air, Roessler began cruising about 800 feet above the surface about a mile from shore when he spied something that looked a little like a raft, then he thought that it might be a kayaker. But, as he got even closer, he gradually realized that it was Bob with one of the life vests that he had dropped earlier. At first, Greg was not visible, but in the next moment his head bobbed to the surface as well.

Rick Roessler jumped on the air as fast as he could and began yelling into the microphone, "I've got 'em! I've got both of them! I'll circle around overhead while you guys come and pick 'em up!"

Although the two waterlogged pilots were exhausted and already starting to suffer from the onset of hypothermia, they ecstatically realized that their buddy Baja Ricky didn't let them down when the going got tough. A few minutes later, Greg and Bob drank in the blessed sight of Ted standing at the bow of the approaching panga with his arms outstretched.

Important Travel and Activity Information

8

WARNING: When driving in Baja California, Mexican auto liability insurance coverage is a must!

Baja Travel Clubs and Mexican Auto Insurance

In the event that you become involved in an auto accident of any kind, it is vital that you understand that Mexican authorities do *not* recognize automobile liability insurance that is written by companies in foreign countries, no matter how widely recognized or prestigious the company may be. You can save yourself a plethora of potential legal problems by making sure that you possess current liability insurance from a reliable Mexican insurance company every time you plan to drive a vehicle south of the border.

For those who may be driving into Baja California only on rare occasions, Mexican auto insurance is most economically purchased on a daily or weekly basis, depending upon the anticipated length of stay. However, residents of California, Arizona, or other nearby states who have friends, property, or business interests in Baja that prompt them to visit on a much more regular basis might want to consider joining a Baja travel club. These operations not only offer a wealth of support and information about all aspects of travel south of the border, they also specialize in offering yearly auto insurance policies that are far more economical than buying insurance on a piecemeal basis. There are basically two major Baja clubs that perform this type of service.

The first such club to be established, Vagabundos Del Mar, has been serving this niche market for decades and also offers special caravan outings for its members, most of which cater to the RV set. The most recent entrant into the field is the Discover Baja Travel Club, which aggressively focuses on the new generation of Baja discoverers who may be more likely to fly or drive into Baja to stay at an upscale resort or remote ecotourism facility, or might have a mind to book the fishing trip of a lifetime in a place like Los Cabos, La Paz, or Loreto. I have personally done business with both clubs over the years, and can attest to their professional performance; but at the same time, I strongly recommend that you select the one that best suits your personality and lifestyle.

An Important Note of Warning to Drivers Insured by AAA

Regular visitors to Baja California who happen to hold auto insurance policies written by the Amerian Automobile Association (AAA) particularly its Southern California entity, are advised to take note of this important fact. Although your policy may state that your vehicle is covered for theft south of the Mexican border, I know from personal experience that this is not always the case. Any claim involving your car being stolen in Baja may be summarily denied if there is a subjective determination by AAA's Theft Claims Department that your travel into Mexico is deemed to be on "too regular" a basis.

Caveat emptor (let the buyer beware) is a key adage to consider when purchasing any insurance plan from a US-based company that claims to cover your vehicle from damage or theft when you are even a few miles south of the border.

Other Tips

Author James Truett is well known for his detailed suggestions in *50 Things You Must Know Before Traveling to Mexico* and, while I applaud his attention to detail and absolutely concur with his well-published synopsis, I honestly think that we can more easily break things down to one simple axiom: No matter where you happen to be, don't take yourself too seriously, and always try and do your best to treat others the way that you would like to be treated yourself!

This means that every time you visit Baja, or anywhere else in Mexico for that matter, you have an opportunity to be an unofficial ambassador for the image of the likable—rather than the ugly—American.

Ugly Americans make it a point to think and act as if they are better than other people, especially those who may happen to have fewer material possessions than they do. Without even saying a word, they often let their feelings be known with their sometimes arrogant or condescending manner when dealing with local vendors, hotel staff, waiters, and residents.

Remember, a friendly smile or a warm greeting always goes a long way where such things are still important, and the Republic of Mexico is one of those places.

Local Pay Phones

Many pay phones south of the border no longer accept coins for security reasons, and instead relay on a prepaid card system. These cards are readily available at most retail grocery outlets and range in cost from 30 to 100 pesos (approximately $3 to $10). The cards can also be used for international calls at rates that hover around $1 to $1.50 per minute. This is expensive, but still cheaper than international phone rates at hotels and resorts. Beware of pay phones that say they will accept your regular credit card! The offer may sound convenient, but they have been known to result in huge bills for unsuspecting callers who end up feeling the sting of the exorbitant charges once they return home and receive their credit card statements.

Dealing with the Authorities and Police Officers

Sadly, almost everyone has heard at least one horror story about tourists being rousted by Mexican police officers who have hit them up for heavy bribes, known as *mordida* in Mexico, which literally translates to "the bite." While these types of activities were much more likely to occur well before the turn of the new century, the practice still occasionally takes place, although recent efforts by national authorities and the Mexican Department of Tourism have drastically cut down the number of complaints, particularly on the Baja peninsula.

Nonetheless, I probably couldn't give any better overall advice to those who are particularly concerned about this phenomenon than does Larry "Lorenzo" Biedebach, owner of the Campo Lorenzo Skypark in San Quintin, Baja Norte.

Offers Biedebach: "If you plan to drive in Mexico, a donation of only $25 to help support the efforts of Sindicatura will probably be the best investment you've ever made. The Sindicatura is a Mexican government organization formed to fight corruption among public officials—including the cops!

"S.O.S, or 'Support of Sindicatura' was formed to assist in these efforts, and it's working. Since recommending SOS, we're receiving lots of stories from people describing how cops suddenly decided not to pull them over when they noticed their affiliation with Sindicatura after seeing the decal.

"Your donation will get you a nice membership packet, but the best deal is the window decal. The Sindicatura decal, to a Mexican traffic cop, is like a cross to a vampire! When the decal appears on the rear window of your RV, truck, or car, any crooked police officer knows that your support of Sindicatura means trouble for him."

I recommend that anyone who drives in Baja on a regular basis simply send a $25 donation to S.O.S. or "Support of Sindicatura" at 7349 Milliken Avenue #140–234, Rancho Cucamonga, CA 91730. Or e-mail them at sosindicatura@hotmail.com. Allow two weeks' turnaround time to get your complete membership package.

For those less frequent visitors driving in Mexico who are stopped and believe that they are not being treated fairly, I suggest that they insist on going to the local "transito" office to pay their fine, or insist upon seeing a superior officer. Quite often, an officer involved in inappropriate behavior will completely drop a charge if he sees that you won't be easily intimidated into paying his mordida. But also be prepared for him to call your bluff, in which case you can probably plan on spending a lot of extra time waiting around at the police station until your situation is addressed. It's a gamble, but one that you'll often win if the officer's allegations are spurious.

Of course, the best tactic to avoid problems with police anywhere in the world is to stay away from any situations that could potentially trigger a criminal charge. While Mexico can indeed be a land of festive revelry, if you plan on drinking and partying, simply don't go overboard and make a spectacle that might draw negative attention to yourself.

Don't Forget The Water!

While I can't emphasize enough the need for those driving down the Baja peninsula to make sure that their vehicle is in good repair, and that they have a toolbox, first aid kit, and cell phone or VHF radio, as well as all the other equipment that might become necessary during an emergency, one of the most important things to have plenty of is water.

You can live for weeks without food, but under the blazing Baja sun you will be lucky to survive for even two days without water. Always take along a few gallons of potable water for each person traveling in your vehicle. Also remember to stay with your vehicle if you should break down. Even on Baja's most remote dirt roads, someone is usually bound to happen upon you sooner rather than later. Unfortunately, the desert sands of Baja have claimed the lives many who did not heed this advice.

If you happen to have car trouble on the main highway, however, you are likely to be helped out of your dilemma by an angel—a Green Angel, that is!

Los Angeles Verdes, or The Green Angels, live up to their name every day of the year along Baja's highways. Their bright green repair trucks can often be observed cruising areas throughout the peninsula in search of motorists in distress. They can fix or change tires, perform certain minor repairs, provide emergency gasoline, and sometimes even tow or push you to a garage or other facility.

When you have car problems along the Baja highway, keep an eye out for this "angel" in green. (LOS ANGELES VERDES)

Try to pay them for their assistance? "No, gracias, amigo!" they will say. This service is provided by the Mexican government in the interest of public safety and with a genuine concern for assisting those who are in need of emergency help on the road.

Fishing In Baja: Know The Rules

Although a fishing license is not required in Mexican waters when fishing from land or from a land-based platform, all anglers fishing in any type of boat, kayak, or raft must have a valid Mexican sport fishing license. This license covers all types of fishing and is valid anywhere in Mexico, and may be purchased for a day, week, month, or year. Everyone aboard any private craft that is in Mexican waters must have a fishing license if there is any fishing gear, fish, or fish parts aboard. This even includes children, regardless of age. For people fishing on charter sport fishing boats, the boat operators normally provide licenses, but always check before you go out on any such excursion. A fishing license is also required for underwater spearfishing.

If you bring your own boat, you will need both a permit for the boat itself and individual fishing licenses. To obtain boat permits and fishing licenses, contact the Mexican government's CONAPESCA (Comisión Nacional de Acuacultura y Pesca) office in San Diego, California. You will need a copy of your valid boat registration to obtain a boat permit. You need not live in the San Diego area in order to buy fishing licenses and boat permits from CONAPESCA. Contact:

> CONAPESCA
> Oficina de Pesca
> 2550 Fifth Avenue, Suite 15
> San Diego, CA 92103
> Phone: 619-233-4324
> Fax: 619-233-0344

Only one rod or line with hook is permitted in the water, per person, but there is no restriction regarding the number of replacement items. The Mexican fishing license allows you to capture only finfish. It does not allow you to capture any mollusks or crustaceans, and their capture by anyone is strictly prohibited. Totuava, turtles, and marine mammals are under the strict protection of the Mexican government, and may not be captured at any time.

To capture bottom fish, up to four hooks on a vertical line may be used. The use of electric reels is restricted to disabled fishermen only, after written authorization from the Oficina de Pesca before use.

In all ocean waters and estuaries, the limit is a total of 10 fish per day, with no more than five of a single species, except for marlin, sailfish, swordfish, and shark, of which only one specimen of any is allowed. The single specimen counts as five toward the overall 10-fish limit.

If you catch dorado, roosterfish, shad, or tarpon, only two of each species are allowed, and these two count as five toward the overall 10-fish limit. The limit on inland bodies of water (rivers, lakes, dams, etc.) is five fish per day, whether of a single species or in combination. Underwater fishing is limited to five fish per day, using rubber band or spring-type harpoons, and only while skin diving without the aid of scuba gear. There is no limit to the practice of catch-and-release, as long as any fish that exceed the bag limit are returned to the water in good survival condition.

Where sport fishing is conducted from boats out at sea for longer than three days, the bag limit is the equivalent of three times the numbers mentioned above.

It is illegal to sell, trade, or exchange any fish caught. Fish should not be cleaned at sea, but should be brought to fish cleaning stations at the marinas. Fish can be eviscerated and filleted, but a patch of skin must be left to permit species identification.

The taking of abalone, lobster, shrimp, clams, cabrilla, totuava, oysters, and sea turtles is prohibited. Purchases of these species may be made at designated public markets or fishing cooperatives.

Additional Regulations

It is illegal to capture and maintain alive any fish for ornamental purposes.

It is prohibited to receive any financial gain from the product obtained through sport fishing.

It is prohibited to dump trash, litter, or substances that harm the aquatic flora or fauna, whether on lakes, river banks, shores or oceanic waters.

It is prohibited to collect shells, corals, sea anemones, and snails, or to disturb the original ecosystem.

It is prohibited to practice sport fishing 250 meters or less from swimmers.

It is prohibited to use artificial lighting to attract fish.

It is prohibited to discharge firearms in Mexican waters.

Any fish caught under a sport fishing license may not be filleted aboard the vessel from which it was caught.

It is requested that all unusual activities, occurrences, or record catches be reported to the nearest office of the Oficina de Pesca, or to its representation in San Diego, California, in order to ensure the preservation of natural resources for the continued enjoyment of all fishermen.

Note: Sea turtles are protected under Unites States law and may not be brought into the US. Be prepared to show your Mexican fishing license to US Customs if you plan to bring your fish back into the United States.

Baja Mileage Chart

Tijuana																			
12	*Rosarito*																		
68	56	*Ensenada*																	
120	108	52	*San Vicente*																
184	172	116	64	*San Quintin*															
221	209	153	101	37	*El Rosario*														
297	285	229	177	113	76	*Catavina*													
362	350	294	242	178	141	65	*Punta Prieta*												
405	393	337	285	221	184	108	43	*Bahia De Los Angeles*											
443	431	375	323	259	222	146	81	124	*Guerrero Negro*										
533	521	465	413	349	312	236	171	214	90	*San Ignacio*									
579	567	511	459	395	358	282	217	260	136	46	*Santa Rosalia*								
618	606	550	498	434	397	321	256	299	175	85	39	*Mulege*							
703	691	635	583	519	482	406	341	384	260	170	124	85	*Loreto*						
794	782	726	674	610	573	497	432	475	351	261	215	176	91	16	*Cuidad Constitucion*				
926	914	858	806	742	705	629	564	607	483	393	347	308	223	148	132	*La Paz*			
974	962	906	854	790	753	677	612	655	531	441	395	356	271	196	180	48	*Todos Santos*		
991	979	923	871	807	770	694	629	672	548	458	412	373	288	213	197	65	116	*Los Barriles*	
1039	1027	971	919	855	818	742	677	720	596	506	460	421	336	261	245	113	68	48	*San Jose del Cabo*
1059	1047	991	939	875	838	762	697	740	616	526	480	441	356	281	265	133	48	68	20	*Cabo San Lucas*

Buying Property and Living in Baja

It is a common dream: a seaside home with a stunning coastal view far from the complications of urban life, a place where peace of mind is more easily accessible. Unfortunately, for those living in the United States, these types of residential properties are increasingly difficult to find, and when available are generally priced far beyond the budget of an average buyer who is in search of a viable real estate investment.

This is particularly true in Southern California, where longtime residents have witnessed a steady stream of new buyers from outside the region driving prices through the roof, and making the vision of a home with an ocean view virtually unachievable to all but the very wealthy.

Small wonder that many of these same people have begun searching for a safety valve, a venue where they can enjoy a quality of life that was once commonplace along California's southern coast during the middle of the last century. To many, the friendly aura of the Baja California peninsula has become a warm, beckoning oasis where the dream of a relatively carefree seaside existence is far more easily attainable.

A growing number of new condominiums and other developments designed to cater to Americans seeking a residential or retirement villa south of the border now punctuate the busy toll road that runs along the coast south of Tijuana. There are two upscale golf courses along the trek as well: Real Del Mar, located just north of Rosarito Beach, and Bajamar, which is situated about 15 miles north of the port city of Ensenada.

Between these points, bulldozers crisscross the chaparral on a hill just across the road from the celebrated lobster village of Puerto

Nuevo, where throngs of hungry turistas are bused in to eat their fill of one of Baja's most popular crustaceans. They are in the process of creating streets, between which even more housing developments will be built.

This new land rush is already funneling billions of dollars into Baja California's economy, and all the signs point to the probability that this is just the beginning. In previous decades, most of the Americans moving to Baja California were of retirement age, but this is no longer the case. The demographics slice across the board, and include professionals such as physicians, architects, and attorneys.

Baja's culture has become so homogeneous with that of southern California that it is often difficult for many visitors to accept the fact that they are actually in a foreign country. Vendors and locals frequently speak English well, and the United States dollar has practically supplanted the Mexican peso in some areas.

When looking for the right parcel to purchase south of the border, it is important to remember that, in Mexico, there are no licensing laws regulating real estate brokerage or the related sales thereof. Hence, almost anyone can offer property for sale. Although the market may be a bit more aggressive in popular coastal areas, potential buyers can expect to pay about 8 percent in sales commissions to the brokers who handle their purchase.

Unfortunately, well over a decade ago, American newspapers and airwaves were filled with vivid stories focusing on foreigners who had been unceremoniously evicted from homes and property that they had purchased in Mexico. One of the most highly publicized incidents involved a number of beachfront residents near Punta Banda, just south of Ensenada.

Most of these individuals paid money to a local agrarian cooperative known as an *ejido,* which did not actually hold a deed to the land. Sadly, these new buyers also failed to conduct an official title search, and were eventually left in the lurch when the Mexican courts understandably ruled that the actual titleholder was the true owner the land.

Since that time, the Mexican legislature has amended the country's constitution so that foreigners are now allowed to set up a bank trust, known as a *fideicomiso,* and also to form private corporations. This change in policy now makes it possible for noncitizens to enjoy all the benefits of property ownership near the shoreline, which was previously forbidden.

Under a fideicomiso (pronounced fee-day-com-EEE-so), a 50-year

New housing developments continue to expand along Baja's beachfront properties. (LYNN GATCH)

Mexican bank trust is created, which may be extended later for an additional 50 years. While the actual legal title to the property is held by the bank, the beneficial use option is held by the buyer of the property. Similar to trust agreements created north of the border, a fideicomiso may be used by both Mexican and foreign landowners to protect their interests, as well as to determine and name multiple or successor owners.

The initial setup cost of any given fideicomiso is generally based upon a predetermined percentage of the assessed value of the property. After the fact, a nominal annual service fee is also paid to the bank for its ongoing role as trustee in the relationship.

Another way of securing ownership of Baja property is through the formation of a Mexican corporation. This is much easier to do now than it was before the presidency of Vicente Fox, whose party made it possible for foreigners to own a corporation in their country without the previous need for a Mexican citizen's participation as a controlling partner. Still, the administrating foreign proprietors of this entity do not actually own the property themselves—it is owned by their corporation.

Those who would view the formation of a Mexican corporation as a way to skirt the fideicomiso's setup and maintenance fees, and to avoid the 50-year renewal of the bank trust, should do so with caution.

If you do not truly plan to conduct some sort of business or commercial enterprise in Mexico, you will have no legitimate basis for incorporating and will ultimately find yourself with a host of somewhat expensive legal decisions to make.

That said, an entrepreneurial mentality is welcomed in Baja, particularly from those relocated Americans who have good business and consulting skills, and who will help make a positive contribution to the local economy. However, if you are not retired with a supplemental income and have visions of working for a Mexican-owned business as an employee, you might want to reconsider your plan.

First of all, compared to what Americans and Europeans are used to making, the wages for labor in Mexico are extremely low, hovering around $5 a day. Additionally, the Mexican government fully realizes the enhanced employment opportunities that exist in high-profile travel destinations like Ensenada, La Paz, and Cabo San Lucas. They work extremely hard to see to it that the vast majority of these jobs go to certified Mexican nationals. Workers come from all over Baja and mainland Mexico to vie for jobs in Baja's top tourist towns. As a result, foreign applicants have a marked disadvantage when trying to compete.

Despite all the logistical complications involved in moving south of the border, the most important question that anyone who is considering relocating to Baja must seriously ask themselves is rather straightforward: "Is this really a place that I will enjoy living for a prolonged period of time?"

For snowbirds, the mild winter weather is a big draw, while former Southern California residents may also appreciate it, but are already a bit spoiled by the climate they enjoyed while living just a few hundred miles to the north. Come summertime, however, the intense Baja sun begins to take its toll. Inland temperatures, even near the coast, can often be measured in triple digits. At the southern tip of Baja Sur, the high humidity, along with the active hurricane season in late summer and fall, can be daunting to all but the hardiest of souls.

Another factor to consider is the escalating price of real estate as more and more Americans decide to make the move south. Places in Baja California that have traditionally been targeted as potential locales for future residence are now seeing land and housing prices skyrocket at an unprecedented rate.

These areas include, but are certainly not limited to, Rosarito Beach, Ensenada's Punta Banda peninsula, Mulegé, Loreto, San José del Cabo, and Cabo San Lucas. And prices promise to rise even higher as more buyers reach retirement age and begin looking for an escape hatch from the rising costs, congestion, and social deterioration that are now somewhat extensive in the United States.

Another particular that many people may not contemplate when considering moving south of the border is the issue of health care. Although things in this regard are improving rapidly, and prescriptions are often more easily and inexpensively filled in a Baja farmacia than in a California drugstore, the actual treatment you receive may not be as available, or of the same standard, as what you have become used to. On the other hand, dental services in Baja are usually of excellent quality and low in cost.

If the foregoing caveats have not yet deterred you from being interested in learning more about creating a new life south of the border, then you just might be a potential Bajaphile! You will now need to begin arming yourself with as much information as possible, and making sure that you execute everything in this sometimes complicated, often confusing process correctly.

Title Ownership

In addition to retaining a competent attorney to handle the finer points of a Baja real estate transaction, foreign buyers should also consider taking out title insurance policies on their potential investments. Two well-respected firms that currently handle such indemnities in Baja are Stewart Title Guaranty Corporation and First American Title, which are names already familiar to most Americans, and as such have established professional images that to help to inspire a sense of security in new investors.

Because actual title ownership can sometimes be a bit ambiguous on properties in Baja California, it is a decided advantage, prior to making a purchase commitment, to secure the services of a professional title insurer who will diligently undertake the exhaustive search of related property records for you.

Sometimes, this process requires going back several decades to be able to establish the clear title holder. And having a good title insurance policy also protects the buyer from becoming involved with property that has unpaid taxes pending, or any similarly undesirable obligations attached to it.

Lic. Manuel Fernandez and Guillermo Valencia are partners in the prominent Tijuana law firm of Fernandez & Valencia (www.lawmx .com), which is located in the city's Rio district and regularly handles a wide variety of legal procedures related to foreign investment in Mexico. They are also two of only a handful of attorneys who are specifically trained and certified in matters involving real estate purchases in Baja made by groups and individuals outside the country. In an effort to clarify any confusion about acquiring land in Mexico, they offer answers to a few of the most frequently asked questions.

What is the most common misconception that you encounter with new clients from the United States regarding their understanding (or misunderstanding) of Mexico's land ownership laws?

"I think that the most common misconception is that they expect business will be conducted here the 'American way,' and they then get frustrated when dealing with the manner in which things are done in Mexico. We have a more formal system that puts more emphasis on the written accord.

"In addition, our bureaucratic apparatus is sometimes much less efficient than in the United States. This is another reason why getting good legal advice is so important. You have to consider that our common law system and the Spanish civil system are completely different legal institutions.

"For example, our notary and registration system: in Mexico, a notary public is an attorney with a state or federal license to advise both parties with neutrality and draft instruments that are considered public documents. In order to properly close a real estate transaction, you need to have a notarized agreement and register and submit it before the Public Registry of Property; it has to be a notarized instrument."

What actual ownership rights for foreign real estate investors are included in the bank trust configuration known as the fideicomiso?

"Their ownership is not on the property itself, since they cannot actually *own* any. Rather, they own beneficiary rights on the property derived from the trust.

"The fideicomiso, or bank trust, is an institution adopted from the common law system, and is very similar to a trust in the United States. It is an extremely versatile contract; it can be used for estate planning or as a vehicle to guarantee financial obligations, but the most common type of fideicomiso that we see along the coast of Baja is the real estate trust.

"The real estate trust enables foreigners, who are technically prohibited from owning property in the restricted zone one hundred kilometers from the international border or fifty kilometers from the coast, to legally act as owners. They can then build and live on the property, lease it, sell it, and even inherit it."

When is the formation of a Mexican corporation an appropriate vehicle for land ownership in Mexico, as opposed to obtaining a fideicomiso?

"The Mexican foreign investment laws expressly prohibit direct acquisition by a Mexican corporation with foreign investment of properties that are destined solely for residential purposes.

"If, however, the entity in question is also going to set up a business, or use the real estate for industrial purposes, then direct acquisition of the property by a Mexican corporation may be recommended."

Is there any land in Mexico that can be purchased outright by foreigners without the need for a securing a fideicomiso or forming a Mexican corporation?

"Yes, if it located outside of the restricted zone. But, since the border is just to the north, and Baja California has the Pacific Ocean on the west and the Sea of Cortez immediately to the east, the entire peninsula happens to lie within this zone."

Do you generally suggest that your clients also purchase title insurance on the land that they purchase in Mexico, or are there some situations where it is not necessary?

"Yes, we do recommend it! The registration and notary system gives the purchaser legal certainty, while the title insurance provides economic certainty. Also, if you seek insurance before acquiring the property, you will then know exactly what you are buying before you invest."

There are many companies now claiming to offer title insurance for property in Mexico. In your professional opinion, which one of them so far has the best track record for good customer service?

"The ones we have been working with are Stewart Title and First American Title; they are both very professional. I also believe that other companies, such as Fidelity Title and Chicago Title, are in the process of coming to Baja California as well. It really all depends upon our client's preference."

What is the most common pitfall for American real estate investors trying to buy land in Mexico?

"The most common pitfall presents itself when potential buyers don't do their homework. You have to seek legal advice in order to make a due diligence or title study of the property in question.

"Another institution in Mexico is the ejido, which is an institution dating back to the 1930s, when President Lázaro Cardenas passed land reform legislation that seized land from former haciendas and other vast, private landholders, and turned them into communal, collective land. Since the constitutional amendments passed in 1994, however, ejido land may now be reverted into private property after execution of the proper legal procedures."

If you had one single piece of advice for foreign investors in Mexican real estate, what would it be?

"Once again, it is essential that buyers do their homework and seek professional legal advice before entering into any type of agreement to purchase property in Mexico—or anywhere else in the world for that matter! If you are told by a seller, or an agent, that 'this beautiful piece of land on the border' or 'this lovely house on the beach' does not need to be in a corporation or in a trust, or that it does not need to be closed

A dolphin surfaces near a moored boat in a Baja cove. (LYNN GATCH)

by a certified Mexican notary, we advise you to walk away immediately . . . and very quickly!"

One thing is certain. Whatever your reasons may be for considering relocating to Baja California or investing in Mexican real estate, you are likely to encounter better overall property value and investment growth potential, a high percentage of affordable coastal properties available, a lower cost of living, a lower per capita crime rate, and—perhaps most important of all—a better quality of life.

Here, there are countless opportunities for a fresh new start in a magical world where dolphins play and lines of pelicans can regularly be observed silently gliding mere inches above the pounding surf.

Index

Page numbers in italics indicate illustrations.